The Incredible Pierpont Morgan

The Incredible Pierpont Morgan

Financier and Art Collector

CASS CANFIELD

Harper & Row, Publishers
New York Evanston San Francisco London

Designed and produced by George Rainbird Ltd,
Marble Arch House, 44 Edgware Road, London W2, England
House editor: Penelope Miller

Text filmset by Oliver Burridge Filmsetting Ltd, Crawley, Sussex, England
Text and color plates printed by Amilcare Pizzi, Milan, Italy
Book bound by Dorstel Press Ltd, Harlow, Essex, England

Library of Congress Catalog Card Number: 73–15000
ISBN 0–06–010599–2
Printed in Italy for Harper & Row, Publishers, Inc.
First published 1974

To my son, Cass

CONTENTS

COLOR PLATES

AUTHOR'S NOTE

As a small child I would look out of the window of our house on Thirty-sixth Street and Park Avenue and gaze at J. Pierpont Morgan's house at the corner of Madison Avenue. Although I don't recall ever having met Mr Morgan – I probably would remember if I'd encountered that striking personality – my mother would tell me about her conversations with him.

After the Morgan Library was built between Morgan's house and ours, my family moved uptown and I forgot about him. But when I was sent to the Institut Sillig in Vevey, Switzerland, I felt his presence again, since he had been a pupil there some fifty years earlier.

Upon graduation from college I had no clear idea of what I wanted as a career. It was by chance that I found my way into book publishing, having first looked for a job with J. P. Morgan & Company. I finally settled in with Harper & Brothers and discovered that about twenty-five years before, Morgan had saved the firm from bankruptcy by lending it, at great risk, over a million dollars, in the belief that the continuance of Harper's was important to the cultural life of the country. For many years Harper's was run by Morgan's appointees – George Harvey, who successfully promoted Woodrow Wilson's Presidential campaign, among them – and it was only just prior to my employment there as a junior salesman that Harper's was reorganized and operated independently.

I knew Thomas W. Lamont, one of Morgan's partners, quite well and Harper's published his delightful book, *My Boyhood in a Parsonage*. Morgan's grandson, Harry Morgan, and I were schoolmates at Groton. So my connections with the great Morgan are many, and this has impelled me to write about him in an attempt to discover the mainspring of the man who became the foremost financier and art collector of his time. Considerable space is devoted to Morgan the collector, partly because that is one of my special interests and partly because that side of Morgan is far less known than his activities in finance and industry.

8

In the course of research I became more and more absorbed in this complicated and driving man. There were many facets to his character – some of them contradictory. His romantic streak was expressed in the search for works of art for his great collection; his practical side was satisfied by the exercise of power and the attainment of a position from which he dominated his competitors.

Of the many books I have used in the preparation of this short biography I feel especially indebted to Frederick Lewis Allen's *The Great Pierpont Morgan* (1949) and to *Merchants and Masterpieces: The Story of the Metropolitan* by Calvin Tomkins (1970). Herbert L. Satterlee's *J. Pierpont Morgan: An Intimate Portrait* (1939) also proved to be an invaluable source.

Members of the Morgan family – Harry Morgan, Mrs Mabel S. Ingalls, Mrs George Nichols (all grandchildren of J. Pierpont) – kindly allowed me to ask questions; and Mrs Sherman Haight and Dorothy Miner – close friends of Belle Greene, Morgan's librarian and curator – also gave me invaluable information. I want to thank Frederick B. Adams, Jr, former Director of the Morgan Library, and Charles Ryskamp, the present head, for important help; thanks also to John L. Weinberg for checking the financial aspects of Morgan's career. And without the assistance of Mrs Nicholas King in the research for this book it would have been difficult to complete. Finally, I wish to acknowledge the help of Elizabeth Lawrence, Beulah Hagen and Richard E. Passmore, who made valuable editorial suggestions.

New York City
March 1973

A cottage sketched by the ten-year-old
Pierpont for his Grandmother Morgan

I

PIERPONT MORGAN'S ORIGINS – HIS YOUTH

UNLIKE MANY of the leading businessmen of his time who started with nothing – John D. Rockefeller, Andrew Carnegie and E. H. Harriman – J. Pierpont Morgan came from generations of prosperous merchants. His grandfather, Joseph Morgan, was descended from stolid farmers and seafaring Yankee traders. Miles Morgan, who landed in Massachusetts in 1636, was the earliest of the family in America; Joseph, with his thrifty wife, Sarah Spencer, moved to Connecticut and bought a farm near Hartford. He arrived when the town was booming; it was on the main line of coaches transporting goods and travellers between New York and Boston. Joseph saw his opportunity and invested in stage lines and roadside taverns. In time he became proprietor of the City Hotel in Hartford, and, by 1835, had made a fortune. He then formed a group which, with some associates, gained control of the Aetna Fire Insurance.

So Joseph's son, Junius Spencer Morgan, the father of Pierpont, was born rich. Junius was handsome, dignified and responsible; a man of strict rectitude with an acquisitive temperament. In contrast, Pierpont Morgan's maternal grandfather, the Rev. John Pierpont, although stern, had great dash and a sense of adventure. At the age of seventy-six he was serving as a chaplain in the 22nd Massachusetts Regiment during the Civil War. When he died he was only a minor clerk in the government bureaucracy at Washington, but he had made his mark as a poet, preacher and reformer. Long before Abolition became popular John Pierpont had advocated freedom for the slaves; he had leanings toward Socialism and opposed the accumulation of great wealth. His poem, 'The Patriot', became justly famous, and on his eightieth birthday he was called upon by a number of friends, who presented him with an album filled with letters of praise from distinguished Bostonians, including John Greenleaf Whittier and Oliver Wendell Holmes.

Descended from two such different strains, it is little wonder that John Pierpont Morgan, born on 17 April 1837, and one of five children, was a complicated character; yet as a boy attending school in Hartford he appeared to be quite ordinary – somewhat taciturn and inclined to have his own way, but not unusual. He did not then excel in any single branch of study. Among his playmates was Jim Goodwin, a first cousin, who became a lifelong friend and an early banking partner of Morgan. Strong enduring attachments were characteristic of Pierpont.

Junius Morgan prospered. He succeeded as a dry goods merchant, became a pillar of the Episcopal Church and a civic leader. His cultivated wife, the daughter of John Pierpont, the poet, encouraged him in cultural pursuits but apparently had no effect upon his rather stiff conservatism. With the expansion of his business, Junius moved to Boston, to the discomfiture of young Pierpont who missed the pleasures of the more rural Hartford. Pierpont – 'Pip', as he was called – entered the Boston English High School at the age of fourteen. Interestingly enough, the subject of his graduating paper was Napoleon Bonaparte. Also significant was his purchase of rubber erasers which the headmaster had sent him out to buy. Pip returned from his errand with more change than the master expected and when asked about the transaction, explained, 'I bought them at the wholesale rate.'

During his school years Pip's health began to fail, he lost weight and suffered from inflammatory rheumatism and headaches; a change to a milder climate was called for. Then an event occurred which affected the future fortunes of the Morgan family: a distinguished-looking gentleman named George Peabody met Pip's father, was impressed with his shrewdness and solidity and offered him a partnership in his mercantile banking firm, George Peabody & Company of London. One of the stipulations of the partnership agreement was that Junius Morgan should take on the responsibility of entertaining for the firm. For this he was allowed $25,000 a year, a very large sum in those days.

When the Morgan family moved to London, they decided to send Pip to the Azores, where they hoped the climate would benefit him. Their friend Charles W. Dabney, the American Consul at Horta, undertook to care for the boy, who was lodged at a hotel nearby. From the Azores Pip wrote long letters to his family, full of meticulous observations on the climate, on the ships coming in and out of the port; he was methodical, too, in reporting upon the temperature at various times of the day. There was also evidence in his letters of an appreciation of beauty; he commented on the view from his window: 'Pico is a very beautiful

Left Pierpont's father,
Junius Spencer Morgan
Below Bagatelle, the
Dabneys' house at Horta

Pip as a schoolboy in Switzerland

mountain and it seems to me as if I should never tire of looking at it. It varies so, both as to clearness and colour.'

On Pip's arrival in Horta, in November 1852, his weight was down to 120 pounds, but four months later it had climbed to 150. Soon after, he took a ship to England, and on this journey he formed the habit of keeping a diary, entering the exact latitude and longitude reached at noon and the mileage of each day's run.

The level-headed, methodical sixteen-year-old boy was turning into a bulky six-footer. He cut an impressive figure with his piercing eyes, and he was handsome, although from time to time he suffered from eruptions on his face. He was not an athlete, but enjoyed walking, riding and climbing mountains. Such were Pierpont's outward characteristics when, after his final year at the Boston English High School, he entered the Institut Sillig in Vevey, Switzerland, in 1854.

Well-mannered and quite experienced for his age, Morgan quickly became one of the leaders in the school. He was possessed of unusual strength – one day he carried to a distant inn a fellow student who had sprained an ankle during one of the excursions the boys used to take in the mountains above Lake Geneva.

The headmaster, Monsieur Sillig, was a keen observer of human nature and took great interest in Pierpont. His first comment on the boy was 'We get on very well', but a little later he noted: 'Adapts himself very slowly. Will not be taken unawares. Smokes.' A few months later Pip fell ill and suffered from fainting spells; when he recovered, he was restless and neglected his studies. Monsieur Sillig was at his wit's end. However, following the summer vacation spent with his family in Paris, Pierpont concentrated on mathematics under Professor Scheiterberg, who was strongly impressed with his ability. In fact the professor said later he was little short of a prodigy; he solved, by mental arithmetic, problems involving cube root and long decimals.

But young Morgan did not spend all his time on cube root; in fact he had a rather wild sense of fun. With a group of friends he organized a series of private subscription dances. These gave him great pleasure, and in a letter to Jim Goodwin he wrote:

> How I have enjoyed myself! They are not those stiff, formal reunions which I so much detest . . . but everything was free and easy . . . The company is very choice and select and everything goes off in capital style. It cost me about $5.75 a night, but that is dog cheap when you can laugh, talk and dance with such a beautiful girl as Miss H. as much as you choose.

The next letter to Jim Goodwin, written from Göttingen in Germany, describes what happened when Pierpont left Sillig's. He says that he stayed on at the school later than planned because the theatricals had been postponed and he wanted to attend the last ball given by his group. The boys had hired a large hall in Vevey and fixed it up like a theatre.

15

Tickets were sold and the Prince and Princess of Prussia were present as well as other notables. The play was a success; the ball that followed lasted until 3 A.M.

He mentions in a letter to his family that he and a friend went to Geneva, where they had some excellent photographs taken. He adds: 'Grandmother will be rather surprised, I know, to hear that anyone with such an eruption on my face should have had their portrait taken.' At that point in his life Morgan was apparently not sensitive about this disfiguration – *acne rosacea* – but in middle life the eruption became chronic and caused him much distress. It made him shy and very reluctant to be photographed; this shyness often made him brusque.

The salient features of Pierpont's character had revealed themselves by the time he left school. Throughout his career the conflict between his homespun Yankee background and his sophisticated continental schooling was constantly breaking to the surface.

The University of Göttingen, celebrated for its courses in chemistry and mathematics, attracted young Morgan, who matriculated there in 1856. The great majority of students were Germans from the various Teutonic kingdoms, but there were also students from Denmark, Sweden and Great Britain, and many from the United States. Pierpont did not join one of those student corps which existed largely for duelling; the facial scars so highly esteemed by its members did not appeal to him. He and his American friends joined a purely social corps called *Konkneipanten*.

Among his American predecessors at Göttingen were George Bancroft, John Lothrop Motley and Henry Wadsworth Longfellow. Morgan found the German language difficult and observed, 'I fear that I shall make bad work of it, but as my maxim in the matter is "sink or swim, live or die", I shall practise the language with the young ladies at dancing parties.' Young ladies again.

Music played an important part in the lives of Germans then as always. Pierpont recalls a garden concert for which tickets were sold for six cents for an excellent performance lasting four or five hours. He wrote:

> These concerts are great concerts for sociability, the fair sex abound in the greatest quantities – the younger portion are engaged in very agreeable conversations with beaux. Plenty of German beer is to be had, and I may as well add that plenty of it is drunk . . .

16

Pierpont spent a short but sociable time as a student in Göttingen.

On one vacation Pierpont travelled to London to join his family, where he had quite a dull time because few American friends were there. So he spent hours in his father's office, sorting and arranging George Peabody's letters and papers. The dull period was relieved by his frequently acting as guide to his sisters; 'They seem to consider me as a kind of "valet de place"!' Then he received news that his trunk, left behind in Göttingen, had been stolen. 'It was very valuable, containing my collections of autographs worth at least $100 – and all the photographs of my friends in Vevey and Göttingen.' A hard blow to the young man and early evidence of his instinct for collecting; among his first acquisitions, incidentally, were the autographs of Episcopal bishops.

Pierpont's life at the university ended in the early summer of 1857. When he said good-bye to Professor Ulrich, his mathematics teacher, he told him that he intended to enter business in America. Ulrich replied that Morgan was making a great mistake, that he should make mathematics his lifework. He assured his pupil that, such was his confidence in him as a mathematician, he would promise him an instructorship and make him his assistant if he would remain another year. He added that he would go so far as to say that he would use his best efforts to have Pierpont chosen as a professor of mathematics upon his own retirement – a very signal honour since, in the view of one historian of science, Göttingen was 'academically speaking the mathematical centre of the world'.

II

EARLY EXPERIENCES IN BUSINESS – MORGAN'S MARRIAGES

MORGAN was enjoying himself in Vienna with Jim Goodwin when he received a letter from his father saying that his friend Alexander Duncan, of Duncan, Sherman & Company in New York, was in London and that there might be an opening in his office for Pierpont if he would return to America at once. Pierpont was introduced to Mr Duncan, who liked him and offered him a job. Duncan, Sherman & Company was well established and had business relations with George Peabody in London; Pierpont was assigned a small desk which looked out on Pine Street in the Wall Street district. Mr Duncan was an expert accountant, and young Morgan's facility with figures made a hit with him.

Not long after he began working for Duncan, Sherman, Pierpont was acting as George Peabody & Company's American representative, selling bills of exchange on the London firm and, in general, acting as its New York agent. In the evenings he would write long detailed letters with candid reports of his business operations to his father in London. (When, toward the end of his life, he came upon these letters, he burned them, fearing that his confidential views on business and the personalities of Wall Street might fall into the hands of a future biographer.)

He led an agreeable life as a young man-about-town; he roomed with Joe Peabody, a nephew of George Peabody, in the fashionable uptown district of West Seventeenth Street, well above Washington Square, then the centre of polite society. In those pre-Civil War days the solid line of brownstone houses reached up Fifth Avenue to only about Thirty-seventh Street; above that were scattered buildings which invaded the market gardens of the Manhattan countryside. Pierpont's account books give some idea of his habits and the cost of living in 1857–8: Lunch 30 cents. Dinner $1. Horse and buggy to Middletown $3. Cap $2. Barber 12 cents. Tickets to the Philharmonic $3. Opera tickets $8. Sleighride $13.62. Supper 37 cents.

Along with his thrift went godliness; he attended church regularly and developed a strong religious faith that lasted throughout his life. The Rev. William S. Rainsford, who became Morgan's close friend, accepted the fact of Morgan's faith only in part and wrote rather bitingly that it was like 'a precious heirloom – a talent to be wrapped up in its own napkin and venerated in the secret place of his soul . . . in safe disuse.' This did not mean, however, that Morgan's religion was just something with which he appeased God on Sundays for ungodly conduct during the week; it meant that, to him, it was as solid as stone, even though most of the time it may have been out of sight and out of mind. Morgan was a communicant at St George's Church; he made many friends among the substantial churchgoing families and threw himself with gusto into Sunday evening hymn singing at the Babcocks, as well as into country walks at the Osborns on the Hudson, and evening gatherings at the Sturgeses, who owned the only grand piano in New York.

With plenty of money and the highest of spirits, Pierpont was the centre of a lively group of young people. His physical strength was extraordinary; one day he was about to return to work from Garrison, New York, when, as the train was pulling out of the station, he jumped to the car window where his friend Miss Babcock was sitting, took hold of the sill and pulled himself in headfirst. Asked why he had done this, he explained, 'Oh, by the time the car steps would have got to where I was standing, the train would have been going too fast for me to get on.'

In 1861 came the Civil War and with it military draft. Because of his fainting spells Pierpont was ineligible, but in any case the accepted procedure of the time for young men who were well-off was to buy a substitute for a few hundred dollars. Nevertheless, Pierpont felt left out – he probably would have liked to join the Union Army.

One might have foreseen for him a very orthodox marriage; but beneath the young man's gruff reserve ran a romantic streak. He usually held this down, but it flared up in his overwhelming love for Amelia Sturges. When she at first declined his offer of marriage, he persisted, and it soon became known that they were to be married; then 'Mimi' caught a cold that settled in her lungs and her health rapidly deteriorated. However, Morgan was characteristically intent on getting what he wanted and succeeded in persuading Mr Sturges that he should marry his daughter and take her to a warmer climate. The

A photograph of Pierpont taken shortly after the death of his first wife, Amelia Sturges *left*. He married Frances Louisa Tracy *below left* three years later.

wedding took place in the Sturges town house in New York; Pierpont had to carry Mimi downstairs where the Rev. Dr Tyng was awaiting them. Supported by the strong young bridegroom, she went through the marriage service. Again her husband carried her, this time to a waiting carriage which took them to the pier on Fourteenth Street to board the steamship *Persia* – bound for Liverpool. From England the couple went to Algiers, where Pierpont determined to forget his career and devote his entire energies to keeping Mimi alive. But despite his tender care she began to fade away. In a final desperate effort to save her, he took her to Nice, where her mother joined them; she remained there until Mimi died, after only four months of marriage. Thus all Pierpont's hopes for a home and children were wrecked, and his pattern of life shattered.

Pierpont's father, Junius Morgan, had objected strongly when Pierpont impulsively abandoned his job to marry Mimi and care for her abroad. At this time Junius had little confidence in his son, whom he considered arrogant, erratic, lacking in talent, with no urge to work, and no spark. 'What shall I do with him?' he complained to a friend.

Forever after, Pierpont kept his impetuousness under strict control, finding outlets in the pursuit of power and in a love of magnificence. A photograph of him at twenty-five, just after Mimi's death, shows a face marked by the tragedy, and there is an intensity in his gaze not revealed in earlier ones. His hair is longish, he has a small mustache now and wears a high stiff collar. As time passed, his spirits were gradually restored; he joined the Union Club, became a member of the board of managers of St Luke's Hospital, was active in the Y.M.C.A. and helped to organize the Metropolitan Museum and the Museum of Natural History. He also became a vestryman of St George's Church in Stuyvesant Square.

Pierpont was now concentrating on business, and his stern father worried less about him. Banking called for great skill in the 1850s and '60s. Railroad construction was developing feverishly and the country was becoming rapidly industrialized. All this required massive amounts of capital, unavailable in the United States; hence it had to be obtained from abroad, mostly from England. This is where George Peabody & Company, the American investment bankers in London, came in. When Mr Peabody retired in 1863, the firm name was changed to J. S. Morgan & Company.

Anxiety in Wall Street on 13 October 1857 as news of the Panic breaks

American industrial progress was then handicapped by alternate periods of prosperity and of severe depressions; the Panic of 1857 almost wrecked Peabody & Company. Unregulated industrial development, overbuilding of railroads, the reckless pile-up of state debts, and frenzied speculation in Western land reaped a whirlwind of economic disaster. It was at this time that Pierpont Morgan was set up independently by his father under the firm name of J. Pierpont Morgan & Company and began representing J. S. Morgan & Company in the United States. The chief function of the father-son combination was to reassure British bondholders that their American investments would be of value in the long run. The integrity and soundness of these two men, apparent to anyone who did business with them, restored confidence in American securities. In fact, had it not been for the two Morgans, European investment in America's railroads and industry would have been far less than it was and the great post-Civil War development of the United States could not have taken place.

In 1865 Pierpont was married again – to Frances Louisa Tracy, an extremely pretty and sweet-natured girl whose father was a leading New York lawyer. Pierpont's father gave her a settlement because he still doubted whether his son was capable of supporting her. With the gentle Fanny, Pierpont settled down to years of brownstone domesticity. She bore him four children: Louisa; John Pierpont, Jr, his successor as head of the House of Morgan, who looked very like his father; Juliet Pierpont; and Annie Tracy, who, as Anne Morgan, was famous for her work in French war relief in World War I. Morgan loved his children and grandchildren but stood no nonsense from them. Once, when his grandchildren were misbehaving, he turned to their mother and said, 'Don't ask them what they want to do. Tell them.'

He prospered in business, reporting in 1864, at the age of twenty-seven, an income of $53,286 – an enormous sum in those days when there was no income tax, but much less than the income of William B. Astor, which was $1,300,000. His business associates of this time said of Morgan that he showed no signs of the extraordinary capacity for handling critical business situations which he later developed, but that he thought quickly in an emergency and acted promptly. Pierpont kept in touch with the movements of the armies in the Civil War and then installed in his office the first private telegraph line in the Wall Street district. This concentration on getting information about what was happening in the world paid big dividends; well into the twentieth century Morgan & Company 'intelligence' was equal, if not superior, to that of any government.

In these eventful early years Morgan became involved in a dubious enterprise – the 'Hall Carbine Affair'. During the Civil War he lent $20,000 to a man named Stevens who was selling outmoded carbines to General Frémont at $22 apiece; they had been purchased from the War Department for $3.50. The deal was scandalous, reflecting gross incompetence on the part of the War Department and greed on the part of Stevens. Much has been made of this episode by certain Morgan biographers, and a legend was started, besmirching Morgan. But the facts are that he did not share in Stevens' profits and that he detached himself from the operation at the earliest possible moment, refusing to lend Stevens further money.

Nevertheless, in his younger days Morgan enjoyed gambling in speculative enterprises – an interest he did not pursue in later years. While still a youth, on a business trip to New Orleans, having heard that coffee was a good 'spec', he bought a shipload which had been consigned to a man who had disappeared. He charged the cost to Duncan, Sherman & Company in New York, from whom he received an indignant telegram ordering him to get out of the transaction as fast as possible. He replied that he had sold the whole cargo at a good profit and that the matter was closed. Morgan liked to do things by himself.

He was, of course, shrewd; but not invariably so. There is a story, possibly apocryphal, which is suggestive of his free and easy purchasing habits. Two men who owned a steel mill decided, as they were walking to Morgan's office, that it should fetch five million dollars. One of them said to the other, 'He's very rich, why don't we ask for ten?' As they entered the office, Morgan said to them abruptly: 'Now I don't want to hear any talk from you men; I know all about your plant and what it's worth; I haven't time for haggling; I'm going to give you twenty million dollars – now take it or leave it.'

N. Y. GOLD ROOM AND STOCK BOARD.

We gave last week's record of the fluctuations of the New York gold market during the memorable 24th of September. These fluctuations were not paralleled during the war period. No such scene as that presented in the Gold Room on the 24th has been witnessed since the Jay Cooke and Chase panic of May, 1864.

The Bulls when they met that morning were confident. Some of them boasted that they could carry gold up to 200. Much of this confidence was due to the fact that the Bulls felt secure as to any interference on the part of Secretary Boutwell. So they blew up their bubble; they carried gold up to 162½, which point it reached at thirty-six minutes past eleven o'clock A.M. Among the prominent operators were Albert Speyer, Henry Clews, Horace Waldo and his brother, Mr. Colgate, of the firm of Trevor & Colgate, Messrs. Kimber & Heiser, and fifty others. In order to bring before the reader's mind the scene of this

THE NEW YORK STOCK EXCHANGE BOARD IN SESSION, SEPTEMBER 25, 1869.

SCENE IN THE GOLD ROOM, NEW YORK CITY, DURING THE INTENSE EXCITEMENT OF FRIDAY, SEPTEMBER 24, 1869.

Black Friday, 1869

III

THE AMERICA OF MORGAN'S TIME

EVERY MAN reflects his time and J. Pierpont Morgan reflected his intensely for he was very much aware, as a businessman, not only of the trends of his period but also of where those trends were to lead. Accordingly, in order to understand Morgan, one must take a look at what was happening during the years he was active – from 1865 to 1909, that is, from the end of Lincoln's administration to the end of Theodore Roosevelt's.

The character of the period prior to 1865 may be compared, in many respects, to that of Robert E. Lee, the civilized Southern gentleman; that of the years following the Civil War, to that of Ulysses S. Grant, the tough, able, hard-drinking general from the Middle West. No two men could have been in greater contrast.

Grant, though a superb military commander, was a sad failure as President (1869–77); he had no conception of how to lead a burgeoning country. Shortly after he assumed office came 'Black Friday', when Jay Gould and Jim Fisk ('Jubilee Jim'), stock manipulators, induced Grant's lobbyist brother-in-law to exert himself to prevent the Government from selling gold. They failed in this shady enterprise, but Gould and Fisk were able to spread the rumour that the President was opposed to sales of gold and profited greatly thereby. When the Government finally did sell $4 million worth, the price plunged from 162 to 135, to the ruin of many. Although Grant could not be held responsible for the stock manipulation, the fact is that he surrounded himself with a number of dubious characters. Later in Grant's administration, a House of Representatives investigation disclosed that William Belknap, his Secretary of War, had taken bribes in connection with the sale of trading posts in Indian Territory.

The country was then a rough-and-tumble place; graft flourished in politics and government; the Tweed Ring was symptomatic of the times. The *New York Times* exposed the regime of Tammany boss Tweed in New York City, where he had seized control of the municipal treasury, which was plundered to the extent of $75 to $200 million through faked leases, padded bills and kickbacks. Little wonder that the business establishment would have nothing to do with politics. But although the political machines were despised as corrupt, they did help the poor and ignorant, opened careers to those with ability and, in general, performed important welfare services. All this for political purposes, of course.

The newspapers of the day were powerful and courageous; they exposed scandal after scandal. In 1872 the New York *Sun* charged Grant's Vice President Schuyler Colfax and other prominent politicians with accepting stock of the Crédit Mobilier (a construction company organized by the promoters of the Union Pacific Railway, to divert to themselves the profits from building that line), in return for political influence. The censure of two members of Congress, after an investigation, proved that the *Sun's* charge had substance. A little later the St Louis *Globe-Democrat* exposed the Whiskey Ring, a conspiracy of revenue officials and distillers to defraud the Government of internal revenue tax. Over two hundred individuals were indicted, including Grant's private secretary, who was saved from conviction through the President's intervention.

In Morgan's time it was the growth of the railroads that caught the public's imagination more than any other business enterprise. Railroads were the key to the development of the country, so it was inevitable that much of Morgan's energy was channelled in this direction. One of the great railroad achievements was the linking up of the line of the Union Pacific with that of the Central Pacific at Ogden, Utah, in 1869, thus establishing rail connections from coast to coast. Congress gave the Union Pacific twenty square miles of land for every mile of track laid; other railroads were given similar huge tracts of land. And so the West was developed; farms and towns sprang up rapidly with a railroad expansion.

The United States was growing from a rural to an urban country – sometimes too fast, causing frequent financial panics. One of the worst was the Panic of 1873 when the powerful banking house of Jay Cooke failed; it was brought about by unbridled railroad speculation and an abrupt fall in farm prices. In the same year occurred 'The Crime of '73', so called by silver mine operators whose mines were rapidly expanding. They objected strenuously to the Coinage Act, which demonetized

The building of
railroads – linking East
and West when the
Central Pacific met the
Union Pacific tracks at
Promontory Point
above – accelerated
development of the
country.

29

silver and made gold the sole monetary standard. The charge that this
act was part of a 'gold conspiracy to ruin the country' had no founda-
tion; nevertheless, this contention became an article of faith for
millions of Americans for twenty years.

It is difficult to realize today how agitated people became over 'free
silver' – they were convinced that dropping the silver dollar from the
coinage standard would debase the currency and make it worthless.
The issue seemed as vital as winning the war against Hitler was to
become in another time. The conflict seesawed back and forth; five
years after 'The Crime of '73' Congress passed legislation providing for
the coinage of silver at a ratio to gold of sixteen to one. Simultaneously
the Greenback Labour party adopted a platform reflecting inflationist
and labour viewpoints, and farmers were pressing for higher prices.

The pressure kept building, and the Populist party Presidential convention in 1892 came out for *unlimited* coinage of silver, a national
currency issued solely by the federal Government – without use of the
banks – and Government ownership of all transportation and com-
munication lines. William Jennings Bryan, the popular orator, became
the leader of the silver bloc in the House of Representatives and in 1896
unsuccessfully ran for President on the issue. His name became
anathema to businessmen.

From Grant through Teddy Roosevelt eight Presidents held office –
all Republicans except for Grover Cleveland and all second-rate except
for him and T.R. Business was in the ascendant; until Roosevelt,
politicians exercised little power and business interests were under no
real controls. Not until 1887 was there any Government effort to
regulate business abuses; in that year the Interstate Commerce Act to
fix railroad rates and investigate complaints finally passed the Senate.
In the absence of federal regulation, legislation within the separate
states had gained momentum, but the Supreme Court virtually stripped
the states of their restraining power. The Federal Interstate Commerce
Act applied only to railroads; it provided that all charges made by them
must be reasonable and that none could be discriminating. The F.I.C.C.
was the first federal regulatory commission in U.S. history. At the out-
set the railroads conformed to the new law but within three years
difficulties in its interpretation made practical results disappointing.

With the establishment of the first industrial combination, the
Standard Oil Trust, the Sherman Anti-Trust Act was enacted in 1890.

The boatloads of motley immigrants who arrived at Castle Garden from Europe and beyond were not always so readily integrated as this cartoon would suggest.

However, this Act was not vigorously enforced, either. Within a dozen years the situation had changed completely; Theodore Roosevelt attacked United States Steel and the Northern Securities Company, a railroad holding company, and directed the Attorney General to file suit for the dissolution of the latter. He pledged strict enforcement of the antitrust laws and strict control and supervision of big business. His 'big stick' was highly effective in the short term.

It was T.R. who coined the term 'muckrakers'; he likened writers like Ida Tarbell, Lincoln Steffens and Ray Stannard Baker, disclosers of shady business practices, to the muckraker in *Pilgrim's Progress* who was so busy raking the filth from the floor that he could look no way but downward. Roosevelt's point was that constructive effort was more important than mere exposure. Nevertheless, the muckrakers, whose writings appeared in the popular magazines – *Collier's*, *McClure's* and *Cosmopolitan* – performed an essential service in directing the public's attention to abuses.

The public at this time was rapidly increasing. Never has there been immigration on a scale comparable to that which inundated the United States in the second half of the nineteenth and first two decades of the present century. The Irish swarmed in following the terrible Potato Famine of 1846–7; also among the early immigrants were the Scandinavians and Germans. The Chinese, too, came in great numbers; it was they who built the Western railroads, while the Irish laboured on the Eastern ones. The end of the century saw the huge wave of immigrants from eastern and southeastern Europe, Italians predominating. It is one of the amazing social phenomena of American history how quickly these millions* became integrated into society and how so many of them became leading citizens.

Inevitably the cheap labour from overseas led to labour troubles. For a long time the immigrants had no voice in labour circles, and indeed the early labour unions took steps to protect their workers from the invasion of unskilled, low-paid labourers. But, as the years passed, the foreigners gradually gained some power.

The National Trade Union Movement, organized as early as 1834, did not gain any real strength until the Civil War was ending. But by

---

*In the decade that followed, when the U.S. population was 76 millions, a total of 8.8 million immigrants arrived on our shores.

32

1872 it had 300,000 members, and the big issue at their meetings was protection against 'green hands'. They were so bold as to demand an eight-hour day, with the result that the State of Missouri enacted the eight-hour day for women and children. The law was not enforced.

In the 1870s violence started. The 'Molly Maguires', a secret organization of miners, promoted it in eastern Pennsylvania, and ten were hanged for murder. There was rioting among the railroad workers in the seventies – in Baltimore, Pittsburgh and Chicago – and President Hayes sent federal troops to quell the violence, which was sparked by Marxian Socialists and Anarcho-Communists. In 1886 the Haymarket Massacre occurred in Chicago; extremists exploded a bomb within the police cordon, with the result that the police fired on the strikers.

The same year saw the establishment of the American Federation of Labour headed by Samuel Gompers. This was progress for labour, but no effective union in the steel industry was formed until the 1930s. At last, in 1905, the I.W.W. (Industrial Workers of the World) appeared on the scene with a platform stressing the need for unionization of unskilled and migratory workers. Another, and very small, landmark for labour was the passage, in 1912, of the first minimum-wage act, in the State of Massachusetts, governing pay to women and minors.

The Negro was at the bottom of the American social totem pole. Although Negroes had been declared citizens, in 1866 their lot was still a sorry one; they were not only denied basic rights but were up against the hate and violence of Southern whites. Within little more than a year after the end of the Civil War the Ku Klux Klan was organized in Tennessee.

Interesting in reviewing these decades are the whispers of the future. In 1876 there existed a Prohibition party sufficiently powerful to nominate a Mr Clay Smith for President. Not long after, the Greenback Labour party endorsed woman suffrage and a graduated income tax. Before the end of the century, Coxey's Army of unemployed marched on Washington demanding a public works relief programme to provide work in a time of deep depression.

America, from 1865 up to the Spanish War, was interested only in herself, in absorbing the immigrants and in the development of the country. No group could have been labelled isolationist because it did not occur to anyone to question the wisdom of George Washington's dictum that the United States should avoid entangling alliances.

35

A Visit to the Nursery by Gabriel Metsu

The 'Molly Maguire' miners *above* and extremists in Chicago *below* contributed to the violence of the 1870s and '80s.

McKinley's high protective tariff cut down international trade, and it was not until Theodore Roosevelt's time that the United States became really 'entangled', although Pierpont Morgan had long been deeply involved with foreign investors and although in his time the bulk of the capital for American railroads and big business came from England.

The big change in the American scene came with Theodore Roosevelt, the progressive Republican trustbuster and the first imperialist-minded President. He had taken part in the Spanish-American War as a Rough Rider. As a result of the peace treaty with Spain, the United States acquired the Philippines, and became an important Pacific power. Roosevelt asserted the authority of government in the regulation of business; his policies led to the imposition of the income tax, which took effect in 1913, the year when the famous Pujo Committee investigated the concentration of financial and banking resources – involving Pierpont Morgan.

The wealth of some Americans in the eighties and nineties was enormous. The new rich built themselves French châteaux on Fifth Avenue and in Newport, and spent lavishly. Charles and Mary Beard wrote in *The Rise of American Civilization*: 'Diamonds were set in teeth; a private carriage and personal valet were provided for a pet monkey; . . . a necklace costing $600,000 was purchased for a daughter of Croesus; $65,000 was spent for a dressing table, $75,000 for a pair of opera glasses.' The parties of the rich were on the grandest scale. In 1897 the Bradley Martins gave a ball in the Waldorf-Astoria, the interior of which was transformed into a replica of Versailles. A member of the Martin family reported:

> I do not think there has ever been a greater display of jewels before or since; in many cases the diamond buttons worn by the men represented thousands of dollars and the value of the historic gems worn by the ladies baffles description. My sister-in-law impersonated Mary Stuart and her gold embroidered gown was trimmed with pearls and precious stones. . . . The suit of gold-inlaid armor worn by Mr Belmont was valued at ten thousand dollars.

Described in the papers with journalistic gusto, the party astounded the country, then in the grip of a prolonged business depression, and brought upon the heads of the host and hostess a storm of invective. In consequence the Bradley Martins sought refuge abroad.

Cornelius Vanderbilt's mansion on Fifth Avenue and Hester Street on the Lower East Side evidence the gulf between rich and poor.

The privileged in fiction and
fact: *above* a Gibson Girl;
right Jenny Jerome

This was the age of the Gibson Girl and of Charles Dana Gibson's
character, the rich Mr Pipp, who looked on while his beautiful daughters
married foreigners of noble birth. There were many such marriages,
sparked by Jennie Jerome, who became the wife of Lord Randolph
Churchill in 1874, by Consuelo Vanderbilt, who married the Duke of
Marlborough in 1895, and by Nancy Langhorne, who became Lady
Astor in 1897.

Part of Fifth Avenue in New York City

Yet despite the grand parties the social scene in America of the nineties was pretty dull; professional men, artists and writers were generally excluded. Dullness did not inhibit Ward McAllister, a Southern aristocrat with a passion for classifying: learning that Mrs John Jacob Astor's ballroom could hold few more than four hundred people, he made up the famous list of 'The Four Hundred' – the only people who could be allowed in Society.

Dreary, too, was the look of New York City, with its endless rows of three or four-storey brownstone houses hardly enlivened by an occasional brown church steeple. The streets were bare of trees and the horse-drawn traffic was congested; sometimes Fifth Avenue would be at a standstill for half an hour on a winter afternoon when the horses slipped and fell on the icy pavements. Yet the city had charm; the smart victorias were elegant, and restaurants like Delmonico's were most agreeable. New York was a big village, lively yet less frenzied than today.

Life was enlivened by such importations as Du Maurier's novel *Trilby*, which sold enormously. Trilby created a vogue; her foot in plaster was hawked in the streets and she created a sudden explosion

Trilby, displaying her admired feet, poses for a sculptor.

In Washington, D.C., a suffragist speaks in favour of votes for women to the
judiciary committee of the House of Representatives.

of the American woman. Woman's suffrage became involved with the
burning question of nude art. Women's freedom was hotly discussed,
and it was maintained that current books contained words unfit for
ladies to read – words like *breast*, *belly*, *damn*, *vomit* and *rape*. In the New
York theatre an English actress, Miss Olga Nethersole, shocked the
audience by permitting her leading man to carry her up the stairs to a
theoretic bedroom at the close of Act I. When the curtain rose again,
he was shown descending in the light of dawn to the accompaniment
of a twitter of zinc birds in the wings. Miss Nethersole was attacked in
the press and arraigned in court for indecency; it was the women, not
the men, who came to her defence.

42

There was much intolerance in the land; an Irish schoolmistress was forced to take an oath that she was not Catholic but really Unitarian. And a committee of Baptists and Methodists in Washington demanded that all Catholic chaplains be withdrawn from battleships. At the time of the Spanish-American War, even Cardinal Gibbons was denounced by a powerful Baptist preacher as an ally of Spain.

Such was America when Morgan was at the height of his career – a turbulent, contradictory, parochial and exciting country bursting at the seams.

Miss Olga Nethersole as Fanny Legrand in Act I of *Sapho* by Clyde Fitch

43

IV

WILD DAYS – THE SUSQUEHANNA RAILROAD DRAMA

DURING THE Reconstruction period railroad wars were at their height and English investors were deeply involved. At this point Morgan and his father stepped in. 'By their courage, determination and integrity they were responsible', in the florid words of Presidential candidate Samuel J. Tilden, 'for upholding, unsullied, the honour of America in the tabernacle of the Old World.' From then on the House of Morgan became a symbol of a decent code of ethics in American business.

These were wild days, when Jay Gould was deliberately wrecking railroads and reorganizing them, unloading their securities on the public and starting all over again. A self-made man, a fighter by nature, he was ruthless. His right-hand man was Jim Fisk, a picturesque adventurer who was famous in the sporting world and the idol of his 'Bowery Boys', known to the Tweed Ring and to every policeman and fireman in New York. He would strut the decks of his Fall River boats, dressed in the uniform of an admiral, ogling the girls. The business practices of these two men were abhorrent to Morgan and he thoroughly disliked them both.

Gould and Fisk together became involved in a bitter struggle for control of the Albany & Susquehanna, a 142-mile railroad connecting Albany and Binghampton and a vital link between the Pennsylvania coalfields and New England. Its president was a man named Joseph H. Ramsey. Gould started buying stock in the Susquehanna, preparing for the annual election of directors in 1869, from which its president had been excluded by court order. In Ramsey's absence one of the directors took possession of his office and locked the doors, whereupon the superintendent of the railroad broke them open again. While William L. M. Phelps, secretary-treasurer, was locked out of the office, the books were removed. That afternoon Phelps was obliged to transfer stock to Gould's nominee.

In August the local sheriff seized the property; the Erie Railroad

Jay Gould *above* and Jim Fisk excelled in
shady business practices.
Below A corner of the rough-and-
tumble Bowery

A violent incident on the tracks

employees were soon running trains at the Albany end of the line, but the Ramsey party was in possession of Binghampton. Neither side dared to run the trains through an intervening tunnel; the hostile forces were stationed at each end. The Erie men attacked and drove the others out, to be ejected, in turn, by their opponents. Many were badly hurt in this encounter and Governor Hoffman called out the militia. The entire countryside was aroused; roughs and bullies, hired by both parties, joined the fray, so that some six thousand men became involved in the struggle. The governor then appointed General Robert L. Banks as executive agent to manage the railroad; at last it seemed that order had been restored.

46

Gould and Fisk were not yet defeated; they were still confident that they could put in their own board of directors at the annual meeting. The bitter struggle was widely publicized and people watched the outcome of the stockholders' election as if it had been a national sporting event. One of the most interested observers was a Mr Samuel Sloan, who disliked both Gould and Fisk; he determined to help Ramsey and his associates with advice. He told them to consult a promising young banker, Pierpont Morgan. Pierpont was sent for and, after hearing the saga of the struggle for control of the Albany & Susquehanna, agreed to try and rescue the road, provided he was given a completely free hand. He bought 600 shares of stock, engaged Samuel Hand for legal advice and took a train upstate to Albany.

The Gould-Fisk forces had meanwhile conspired to obtain an order of arrest to be served on the defendants, Morgan's group, at the hour of the stockholders' meeting. Pierpont had no knowledge of this as he prepared for the meeting and the election of a board of directors. He did not anticipate further violence; in fact, he and his associates would not have known about the strong-arm methods Jim Fisk was preparing to put into effect had it not been for an adventure that befell Morgan's counsel, Mr Hand. Late one afternoon he told Morgan that he was going down to the wharf to see a friend off on the Albany-New York boat, and that he would be back shortly. At suppertime Hand had not returned, and Pierpont waited for him impatiently all through the evening. Finally Morgan went to bed and was awakened in the morning by Hand bursting into his room with the story of his adventure.

He had been so occupied in saying good-bye to his friend on the steamer that he had been unaware of the usual signals that the boat was about to pull out; the first thing he knew, she was on her way down the river to New York. To one ship's officer after another Hand explained that he *had* to get back, but to no avail. In the middle of the night, having become desperate, he made the captain a proposition: he offered to buy one of the steamer's lifeboats. The captain lowered one into the water; Hand climbed in and started to row toward the shore. It was hard going – the lifeboat was heavy and a strong breeze was blowing – but he finally reached land, exhausted. Seeing a light, he clambered over the rocks and reached a railroad station. What a relief! Furthermore, he found that a train to Albany was due shortly. When it passed through the station and stopped at a water tank, Hand climbed up on the rear platform of the last car. He had his hand on the knob of the door leading into the interior when, inside, he saw Jim Fisk and a gang of his plug-uglies from the Bowery; they were drinking and playing cards. Hand beat a hasty retreat to the platform, remaining there until the train reached Albany. 'And that's why I am late', he said to Morgan.

At breakfast, Morgan and Hand were joined by Mr Ramsey. They agreed that what lay ahead was not a legal fight but something like a pitched battle. Their scouts soon located the Fisk forces and a plan was concocted to resist their attack. A few minutes before the hour of the stockholders' meeting Jim Fisk and his gang started up the stairs to the office of the company; when they reached the top, the action began. The portly Fisk was knocked off his feet and fell back on the men who were coming up behind him. Then utter confusion and a free-for-all; the attacking party was taken by surprise and retired in disorder when a policeman grabbed Fisk, placed him under arrest, thrust him through the doors of the police station – and disappeared. The bewildered Fisk found there was no charge against him – the 'officer' was no officer at all, just a Ramsey-Morgan man in a borrowed uniform.

The meeting started punctually. Morgan and Ramsey, hot and dishevelled, entered the office, locked the door and held the election; their ticket won and Ramsey, with his colleagues, remained in office. Pierpont was elected vice president. He returned to New York and leased the Albany & Susquehanna to the Delaware & Hudson Canal Company for ninety-nine years on a seven per cent basis.

This was Morgan's first venture in railroad control. The happy solution of a tangled and violent situation had come about because two determined men had the nerve to stand up to Fisk and his mob; the result was that a long overdue reform era in railroading had begun.

Had the Albany & Susquehanna affair received the direct attention of the resourceful Jay Gould, it is quite possible that things might have turned out differently. But he was devoting all his attention to a market operation in gold from which he profited largely, although it ruined Fisk, who was unaware of Gould's machinations until too late. Fisk had gambled once too often and had brought down on his own head the structure he had built; he went into bankruptcy, together with hundreds of brokers who were forced to suspend payments and close their doors after 'Black Friday' in 1869.

Gould was a ruthless gambler but could be generous under pressure,

The building of railroads across the Great Plains deprived the Indians of millions of acres of land.

as evidenced by his treatment of an old friend who sought his advice about investing $20,000 – all he had in the world. Gould recommended a stock and said it was not only likely to go up but that its dividend was sure. Accordingly, the friend bought the stock, only to find that it declined sharply and passed its dividend. Gould still maintained that it was a sure thing; yet the stock continued to drop. Then the investor stormed into Gould's office shouting that he was ruined and that he had been deceived, and threatening to shoot Gould on the spot. Gould calmly said: 'You are labouring under a most serious misapprehension. Your

49

THE INCREDIBLE PIERPONT MORGAN

money is not lost. If you go down to the bank tomorrow morning, you will find a balance of $25,000 in your name. I sold out your stock some time ago but neglected to tell you.' Half-doubting – and rightly so, for Gould had not sold any shares – the man left the office; the moment he did so Gould sent word to the bank to place $25,000 to the man's credit.*

Victory for Morgan in the Susquehanna affair had added to his reputation, for he had bested two very formidable men – Gould and Fisk. What led to his participation in it was perhaps a trip he took with his wife to the Pacific Coast over the newly finished transcontinental railroad; this was his first visit to the Far West. As they crossed the plains, they saw from the train window a Pawnee war party, herds of antelope, and immigrant trains winding their way slowly westward. All this gave Morgan a fresh sense of the new frontiers for railroads to conquer, so upon his return East he must have been shocked to see the companies demoralized by a senseless battle for control. With his deep sense of order it doubtless seemed to him that the Battle of the Susquehanna was an object lesson in the disorderliness of competition gone hog-wild. Morgan had seen what savage jockeying could do to the railroad industry; it brought corruption, waste, duplication and loss, which were abhorrent to his systematic nature.

In his activity during the Civil War period, Morgan had shown at first an interest in speculative enterprises; and he subsequently had proved his mettle in the Albany & Susquehanna imbroglio. However, he had not yet attained maturity – his aptitudes developed only by degrees. Some people found him arrogant and secretive; he was said to be uncomfortable among equals and repressed among superiors, his impulse being to issue orders and rule.

During the next couple of years he became deeply depressed about his health. He felt perpetually tired, suffered from headaches and fainting spells, and began to think about retirement from business; he had plenty of money to do so comfortably. But this plan ended abruptly when his father engaged in one of the boldest ventures then known to international finance. The French had just been disastrously defeated in the Franco–Prussian War of 1870, with the result that the socialistic Paris

*This anecdote is from *History of the Great American Fortunes* by Gustavus Myers (Charles H. Kerr & Co., 1911).

A folio from *Manafi al-Hayawan*, a Persian manuscript

كه ناه دو سه دوزه پيش كرد الختي ايد تا نخورد وبازهاء كوش بزرگ بيكاز زوبرد وبه خايد

والكر نماز نمود كبي نخورد نيك شود وجوز رغمي خورد از بيزوماند ودد نشماند طلب شعدكذ ونخورد

تا اذرناو برد و زايد والآت اندرونى شير جمله بالآت اندرونى نيك ماند دز افرنش و از خرون نبيد

ومون نبيسد وكازواى كه دد خرون نبيد باشد بر نسل يه كرز نكند واز هيج جنان نكرزيزد كه ازنود

وباد شاهى مونزه بو شر خانت كه بادشاهى ينه بز بيل وبز كا وميش ازناله وباتك نبز نما ت

Commune came into being. At this juncture, Junius Morgan agreed to support the French ministers by floating a $50-million loan to their Government. It was a dangerous gamble, and for the purpose he organized a group of bankers which he called a 'syndicate' – a term that was new at the time. At first the sale of the bonds went poorly and Morgan had to take back quite a lot of them at a heavy discount. Things might have gone very badly for him had not French credit rallied after the war; Morgan's judgment had been vindicated and his firm won for itself in the world of finance a place second only to that of the Rothschilds. The loan proved essential to the stabilization of the shaky French political situation.

Having made a deal of such magnitude, Junius wanted more than ever to have his son in a strong position to sell European securities for him in the U.S. market. And here was that son playing with the idea of retirement! Junius wrote to Pierpont telling him that he had talked to a man named Drexel of the important Philadelphia banking house of Drexel & Company. 'It is possible,' he wrote, 'that Drexel may want to see you about a certain matter.' A meeting between the two took place in Drexel's library, and Pierpont was offered an equal partnership in the firm. He protested that he was in wretched health, but Drexel brushed this aside by proposing that Pierpont take a vacation abroad for one year. On the evening of 1 July 1871, the firm of Drexel, Morgan & Company came into being.

Mr and Mrs Morgan took a steamer to Liverpool and spent some time with Father and Mother Morgan at 13 Princes Gate in London, a pleasant, commodious house overlooking Hyde Park. From London they went to Carlsbad and the Austrian Tyrol. By that time Pierpont had regained his buoyancy of spirit and was able to take long walks over the mountains. On his return to the hotel he would settle into a comfortable chair and try smoking an Austrian meerschaum pipe; but after several attempts he threw it out the window and went back to his innumerable large black cigars, the only form of tobacco he enjoyed.

Following a trip to Rome and the first of many journeys to Egypt, the Morgans returned to Carlsbad. It was there that Pierpont heard that a place called 'Cragston' was for sale in Highland Falls on the Hudson. Cragston was beautiful; built on a knoll overlooking the river and a wooded area through which Pierpont had often taken walks. It appealed to him as an ideal country retreat. Accordingly, he offered to

53

The Duff-Ogilvie portrait of Mary, Queen of Scots, with her son

Mrs Morgan was often happy to stay at Cragston (seen below from the south lawn) while her husband travelled.

Part of Cairo from the citadel

buy it, without any ceiling on the price, and acquired the place. Mrs Morgan was delighted, and they both enthusiastically set about making plans for alterations and furnishings.

They returned to New York for Christmas, which was a merry one, with a tree for Louisa, Jack and the baby; Pierpont was glad to be back for he enjoyed regular habits as well as travel. He liked to know in advance what he was going to do; Saturday was always Whist Club night and Sunday evening was the time for singing familiar hymns, which he did enthusiastically, although the family told him that he couldn't hold a tune. Morgan loved America – yet he had no real belief in democracy. He was really British in temperament. He took not the slightest interest in what came to be called café society and shunned any kind of publicity.

In December of 1876 Morgan took his family to Egypt; he enjoyed Cairo and entertained the children by showing them all the sights.

A family picnic at Karnak. Pierpont is standing with the stick, with Mrs Morgan on his right, Jack on his left, and his daughters, Annie (by the basket), Juliet and Louisa, sitting in front.
Opposite Propylon of the Temple of Philae

Soon after New Year they boarded a steamer he had chartered for a trip up the Nile; they were a happy family party, and Morgan appreciated Egypt more than on his previous visit. He began to be an intelligent collector of antiquities, adding them to his collection of autographs and of broken fragments of stained glass. At Philae, Pierpont put on a grand exhibition of fireworks and fire balloons, to the delight of the natives and of his children. He loved to give shows like this and took endless trouble in preparing them to the last detail.

Although Morgan had been amused by all the sights, he felt nervous and seemed unable to enjoy things quietly. He had to be constantly on the move and felt impelled to entertain everyone he met, at lunch, tea or dinner. Back in Cairo, the party went to hear *Aida*. There was more shopping and sightseeing, more additions to the already large accumulation of jewelry, rugs and scarabaei.

In Paris they stayed at the Hotel Bristol. Morgan took his wife to the dressmaker, Worth, then the best known. One might think that Morgan would make a hurried departure after being greeted by Monsieur Worth. Not at all. He spent hours in the establishment, had decided ideas on materials and styles and took great interest in the selection of brocades and laces. When the time came for fittings, he would make suggestions about the final touches. He even visited Worth's on trips when he was

57

unaccompanied by his family, and ordered dresses to be sent home for them. The unpacking was always an exciting event.

The Prince of Wales, who became Edward VII, was in Paris at the time of the 1877 trip and made the season very gay. Pierpont's father and mother celebrated their son's fortieth birthday by a family dinner party at the Bristol. Shortly thereafter, they all travelled to London, where they enjoyed the Covent Garden opera. Pierpont's favourite was *Il Trovatore*; he was discriminating about the rendering of the different arias but liked only the familiar, romantic, tuneful operas.

Charles Frederick Worth, the *couturier*

Back in the United States Morgan took much pleasure in his farm at Cragston, where he raised Guernsey cattle and collies. Although by the time he was forty he had almost given up riding, he continued to drive a pair of fast trotters and to take long walks. Summer was a busy time for Fanny Morgan – there was much entertaining – but she capably managed the large establishment and was a wonderful mother and housekeeper. She was still as beautiful as when she had married.

The winter of 1878–9 was a brilliant one in New York, which had grown enormously in population and wealth since the end of the Civil War. The Morgans were in the centre of life uptown; they knew the most interesting people and saw and heard the best theatre and music the city had to offer. They had both matured and had reached the prime years of their lives. He had become one of the leaders of the business world.

The year at the office had closed well. As usual, Pierpont stayed there very late – this year until 6 A.M. – to close the books on New Year's Eve. Morgan was tired after a strenuous period and rested. He was a very hard worker, yet he took long vacations and in addition was often obliged to go to bed for a couple of days to get over one of his frequent headaches. The eruption on his nose bothered him, but he was able to

Morgan's first yacht was the *Louisa*, a steam launch.

comment humorously about it: 'It would be impossible for me to appear on the streets without it.' On another occasion he remarked that his nose was 'part of the American business structure'.

Once or twice during the winter he would go to Washington, taking Fanny with him to give her a change; on these trips he would always see the sights and meet the important people there, as had Grandfather Morgan. But he did not inherit his ancestor's fondness for buying real estate; he never claimed to know much about it and, as an investment, it failed to interest him. Nevertheless, he owned houses in New York and London, a camp in the Adirondacks and a fishing box in Newport. And, in due course, an oceangoing steam yacht, the *Corsair*.

59

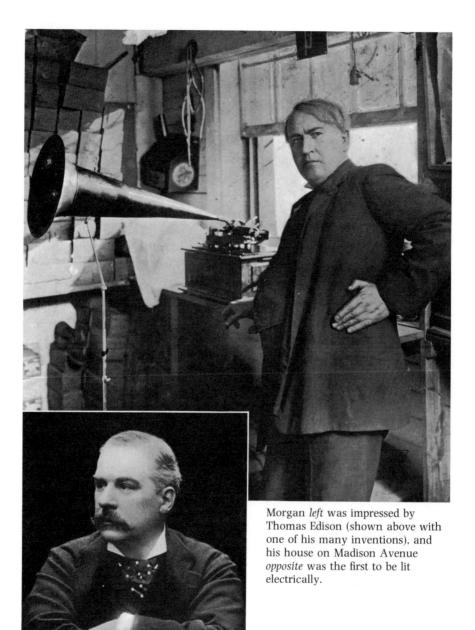

Morgan *left* was impressed by
Thomas Edison (shown above with
one of his many inventions), and
his house on Madison Avenue
opposite was the first to be lit
electrically.

The big newly acquired house in New York was at 219 Madison Avenue on the corner of Thirty-sixth Street, on the northern edge of the residential district. In 1882, having met Thomas A. Edison the year before, Morgan had installed an electric lighting system – the first private residence in the country to be lit throughout with electricity. This was an adventurous undertaking. The installation was difficult, involving the digging of a special cellar for the steam engine to operate the generator. An expert engineer was hired, but there were frequent short circuits and the electric system caused a good deal of trouble to the family.

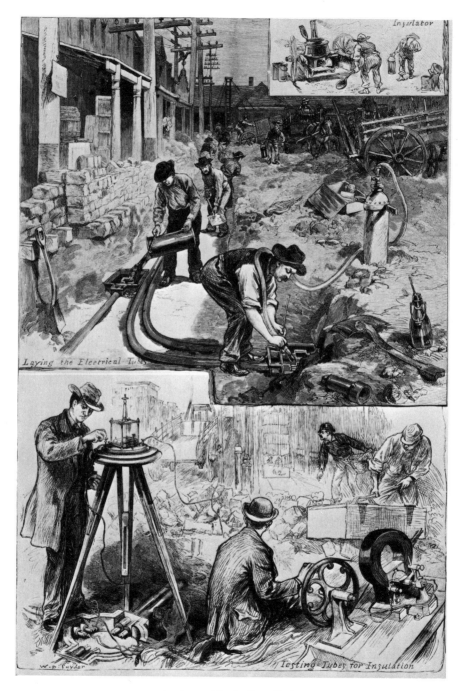

Laying cables in New York

Nevertheless, the installation was a great convenience, especially when initial difficulties had been solved. Pierpont gave a reception to celebrate it, and the four hundred guests marvelled at the new lighting. Among them was the financier D. O. Mills, who told Morgan that he knew all about Edison's invention and was buying Edison stock. Pierpont followed suit and before long had invested heavily in electric securities. Partly as a result of this support, the electric light industry developed quickly and spectacularly.

When Morgan breakfasted at No. 219, he liked to have one of his daughters – usually Louisa – with him, as Mrs Morgan would have her coffee upstairs. With Mrs Morgan he was deferential. She seldom accompanied him on the *Corsair* or on the European trips of his later years. Being shy, domestic by inclination, and in uncertain health as the years went by, she would remain behind at No. 219 or at Cragston while he, with his overpowering energy and love of human society, roamed widely.

Morgan became involved in railroads on a really big scale when William H. Vanderbilt called on him for help. Vanderbilt had greatly extended the railroad properties he had inherited from his father, the Commodore, so that by 1879 he owned three-quarters of the New York Central stock and controlled many of its affiliated and connecting lines. He was a law unto himself; it was he who said, 'The public be damned!' His impulse was to grab while Morgan's was to rule. Things were becoming ominous for Vanderbilt; the people of New York State objected to having their main railroad controlled by one man. At this point Drexel, Morgan & Company bought 350,000 shares of Central for distribution to British and American investors and Morgan became a director.

The New York Central was safe from capture by Jay Gould, but, with George M. Pullman, Gould planned a flank attack that involved building a line that would compete with the whole vast railroad network in the East. The first phase of this railroad war did not attract Morgan's attention, for he was devoting all his energies to banking. But soon he became deeply involved in rails, as Drexel, Morgan & Company underwrote $5 million worth of bonds for the Northern Pacific.

In the summer of 1883 stocks collapsed and the railroads were in a desperate state. There was a near-panic in American rails on the London market. Pierpont resolved to bring order out of this chaos and held a

William H. Vanderbilt's gallery in his Fifth Avenue home

stormy meeting on the *Corsair*, attended by the officers of the principal Eastern railroads and the bankers interested in their securities. George B. Roberts, president of the Pennsylvania Railroad and an antagonist of Vanderbilt, said bitterly that there would be no trouble if the bankers would stop loaning money to build parallel and unnecessary lines. The net result of the conference was the establishment of railroad associations, each one based on a 'gentlemen's agreement', a phrase coined by Morgan.

Morgan and Vanderbilt in a sleigh

V

MORGAN AND THE REV. W. S. RAINSFORD

THE MOST striking thing about Morgan's giving, which was anonymous whenever possible, was the speed of it. Unlike other rich men, especially those of today, he did not rely on committees of experts and had no truck with surveys. He hated haggling and undue deliberation; when he came across something he thought worth giving to, he would do so – at once.

This is what Joseph Gilder wrote about Morgan, the philanthropist, in the *Century Magazine*:

> Harvard University wanted in 1901 to build a new group of buildings in Boston for its Medical School. Morgan liked the idea. Harvard was a good place; his son Jack had gone there and the results had seemed satisfactory. President Eliot was an excellent man. Medicine was a good thing, and the Harvard Medical School was well spoken of. So when Morgan was approached for a gift he said he would be glad to see the plans for the new group of buildings.
>
> ... John D. Rockefeller had taken six months to have the school's needs investigated. Morgan, when two or three representatives of the school came to see him at 23 Wall Street, and were shown into an inside room, walked in, watch in hand.
>
> 'Gentlemen,' said he, 'I am pressed for time and can give you but a moment. Have you any plans to show me?'
>
> The plans were unrolled.
>
> Said Morgan, moving his finger quickly from point to point, 'I will build *that* – and *that* – and *that*. Good morning, gentlemen.' And he departed, having committed himself to the construction of three buildings at a cost of over a million dollars.

Morgan continued his interest in St George's Church, originally the Negro chapel of Trinity Church, and donated to it about one million dollars.* He heard of William S. Rainsford, a forceful and fearless young

---

*Morgan also contributed $4,500,000 to the Cathedral of St John the Divine and over $1,000,000 to the Lying-in Hospital, of which he was president of the Board of Trustees.

William S. Rainsford

clergyman who had achieved success in Toronto as a revivalist. They first met in 1882, when Morgan asked him to come to St George's; he was to have a completely free hand and Morgan promised to find the money to carry out the development plans they had mutually agreed upon. June of 1888 was a happy month for Mr Morgan, who by that time had learned to save his strength by delegating detailed work to his very capable partners, for it was then that St George's parish house, built by him, was dedicated.

Rainsford's parish was large, with a mixed congregation, and he insisted on having it run democratically. He would frequently urge Morgan, the senior warden, to carry out the democratic process by

A portrait of Morgan in 1888

enlarging the number of vestrymen and making them representative of the parish, but got no response. Rainsford, in his memoirs,* writes:

In my weekly talks with Mr Morgan I had many times brought up this subject, but in vain I tried to get a response from him.

This being the situation, I made up my mind to wait a while. I had never found it necessary . . . to bring up in the vestry a matter in which my warden and I were opposed. I always strove to settle such divergency of views 'out of school'.

In 1884, when I insisted on putting the choir into surplices, he almost had a panic, and for a time opposed the move fiercely. Since then we had been a unit at all vestry meetings and, indeed, I usually got him to propose at vestry meetings such measures as I desired carried.

However, it was not so to be in this matter. The vestry met at 8.30 P.M. in the Corporation Room in the Parish House. There, one night, I had the surprise and the fight of my life. I had no hint of what was coming when, ordinary business being over, Mr Morgan rose and said: 'I have a motion to make, Mr Chairman, and I think that the vestry will agree with me it had better be passed without debate.' He then read his motion. It was that the vestry be reduced from eight members and two wardens to six members and two wardens. Having read it, he said: 'I think the vestry will agree with me that when I get a seconder it had better be passed without debate.'

I was fairly stunned . . . but I saw that as chairman I must dominate the situation instantly, or I was undone and my vestry divided. I said: 'Mr Morgan, before I ask for a seconder to your motion, I must say that I think on a matter so important as the alteration of this vestry, you surely should have said something to me of this radical policy you propose before you advanced it here . . . I think you will bear witness that I have never advocated any important matter . . . without first discussing it with you. Here, now, you spring this revolutionary proposition on me, and on the vestry, without any warning whatever; and you ask that we should proceed to pass it without discussion. This I cannot agree to, and I must ask you, before you get a seconder, to explain to me and to this vestry your reasons for proposing so important a change . . . If a small vestry is for St George's a better vestry, there must be reasons for it. What are your reasons?'

Very unwillingly, Mr Morgan got on his feet . . . 'Rector, we are all more than satisfied with what you have accomplished. You have done your part well . . . But this, your vestry, has its part to do. Yours is a

*Story of a Varied Life (Doubleday, Page & Co., 1922)

69

spiritual responsibility . . . The vestry's part is fiduciary . . . I am its senior warden and responsible officer. I am aging. I want at times to have these vestry meetings held in my study . . . The rector wants to democratize the church, and we agree with him and will help him as far as we can. But I do not want the vestry democratized. I want it to remain a body of gentlemen whom I can ask to meet me in my study.'*

The issue was plain; no evading it. If my senior warden was to have his way, St George's vestry would pass under his control. It would not, it could not be, in any true sense, representative of the congregation. In the long fight, for fight it was, which began shortly after nine o'clock and did not end till almost midnight, I did all I could do, all that love for my friend and love for my people prompted, to turn him from his purpose, but I failed completely. And as I opposed that purpose unflinchingly, his anger at opposition rose. Seeing I could gain nothing there, I spoke over his head to my vestry: 'Yes, your obligation is fiduciary, as my warden says, but I protest with all my soul that the main purpose you have been elected to fill is not fiduciary but spiritual . . . Tonight, for the first time since I have been your rector, I find myself in opposition to my senior warden. Mr Morgan has laid his plan for what this vestry should be before you, and you must vote on it. Before you do so, I will as frankly tell you mine. I do not want a smaller vestry. I want a larger one . . .'

I could feel that, as I pleaded with all my soul for a democratic and more representative vestry, I had the support, as yet unspoken, of a majority of those present; but I wanted to win a verdict if possible without a division. I would have done almost anything to save my warden from pushing his motion to certain defeat. 'Will you not withdraw your motion?' I said. 'Do not let us divide; we never had a division on any serious question in this vestry since I sat at your head.'

Here Seth Low, Mayor of New York . . . appealed to Mr Morgan in a moving speech to withdraw his motion. Mr Morgan remained immovable. Then a dramatic thing happened: A member of the vestry, one of his oldest friends . . . slowly rose. He was white to the lips, and, turning to Mr Morgan, said: 'Mr Morgan, I am compelled to agree with our rector fully in this matter, and I move that this vestry be increased to eleven.' Mr Low seconded the motion at once. Mr Morgan would not withdraw but could get no seconder. So I put the second motion, which was carried. The vote stood seven to one.

For a moment we all sat in intense silence. What would this man whom

---

*Morgan made a similar observation when he said, 'You can do business with anyone but you can only sail with a gentleman.'

we all loved and honored do? How take this cruel rebuff, so unwillingly given him? . . .

He rose and, speaking slowly, said: 'Rector, I will never sit in this vestry again.' Then, as all still sat in silence, he walked out . . .

Next day I had Mr Morgan's written resignation, with a request to submit it to the vestry without delay. I acknowledged his letter, and nothing more, going to breakfast next week at 219 Madison Avenue as usual . . . He was very grumpy, and at the breakfast table conversation was limited to the weather. Next week I went again to breakfast; he had nothing to say to me.

As I asked for a cigar, in his study afterward, he said, 'Have you submitted my resignation?'

'I have not, and I will not.'

'Why not?'

'Because I will not now, or ever, put you in the position of going back on your pledge to the rector and the vestry of St George's Church.'

'What do you mean?'

'You know what I mean. When I first came to you I came because you gave me your hand and your promise to stand by me in the hard work that lay ahead. I told you I was a radical. I told you I would do all I could to democratize the church. I am only keeping my word. I certainly shall not now, nor at any time, do anything to help you break yours.'

Dead silence. So I lit my cigar and walked away.

Rainsford and Belle da Costa Greene, curator of the Morgan Collection, were the only people who could stand up to Morgan in a confrontation.

Rainsford continues:

I think that I went to breakfast three times before Mr Morgan sailed for Europe. He never made another allusion to his resignation, nor did he enter into any private conversation with me. The day he sailed, I did what I had not done before, I went to the dock to bid him good-bye . . . He saw me, and coming out of the group, signed to me to follow him. He made for his cabin, entered quickly, without saying a word, and shut and bolted the door behind us.* We never had another falling out.

When he chose to exercise it, there was an extraordinary and winning charm about J. Pierpont Morgan . . . I have never seen any eyes quite like

*Many years later Rainsford told a friend what had happened. Morgan, he recounted, threw his arms around his neck and cried, 'Rainsford, pray for me, pray for me.' From *St George's Church* by Elizabeth Moulton (privately printed, 1964).

his. They had penetration and kindliness combined to an extraordinary degree. When he said a thing, and looked full at you as he said it, I thought him a wonderful man, a man quite in a class by himself, unlike anyone I had ever seen, and I am of that opinion still.

Mr Morgan was a man of faith. His faith was threefold: Faith in himself and his business judgment (when I first knew him I should say that outside of his office, where he was king, he was singularly self-distrustful and diffident. This diffidence passed as years brought him power and flattery); faith in the religion of Jesus, as formulated by the Puritan Calvinistic divines; and faith in the stability and greatness of the United States. He was intensely and unselfishly patriotic.

In religious matters – and he was deeply religious – he had no vision of reforms, and generally little sympathy with reformers. On the religious side of his nature, he was intensely conservative. His beliefs were to him precious heirlooms.

But there was a quality in Mr Morgan that tended to place him among those who stood for advance and reform in religious matters; a quality that balanced the hyper-conservatism of his religious nature – his constant habit of trusting men who did things. He was always looking for men fit to lead. He believed more in men than in measures. Once he found the man he was looking for, or thought he had found him, he gave that man large freedom of action. He was willing to trust him far, and stood ready to defend him bravely and long. Many said, and say, that Pierpont Morgan was a great judge of men. That was not his opinion of himself. Once he said to me: 'I am not a good judge of men. My first shot is sometimes right. My second never is.'

For all the throngs of friends surrounding him, for all the love and fire of personal devotion to himself which he, all unwittingly sometimes it seemed, kindled in his very nearest, he was more reserved than any man I ever knew. When under life's stress that reserve broke down, then the profound emotionalism of his nature had its way with him. The great deeps were broken up, and he called aloud for help.

Pierpont Morgan's was too emotional a nature to escape depression. At times he deeply doubted himself. He had hours, and more than once they were prolonged, of despairing despondency. But such experiences were the result of overstrain and nervous collapse, not of intellectual conviction. Intellectually he was an optimist . . . He was no scholar, no reader, and he had not learned to care for nature, or find any rest or companionship in her high company. So unrest and ennui were sometimes his. Loyalest of friends, he was intemperate and sometimes unjust in his oppositions. Of President Roosevelt he would hear nothing good; when Teddy went to

Africa on his famous big game hunting expedition Morgan said, 'I hope the first lion he meets does his duty.' Yet the two men were made for a fine cooperation.

Lincoln Steffens was an outstanding reporter and his autobiography is a classic of his times. During the Panic of '93 he was assigned to interview a number of private bankers and observed that of these, 'J. P. Morgan was the greatest.'*

I did not see much of him, of course; nobody did. He was in sight all the time. He sat alone in a back room with glass sides in his banking house with his door open, and it looked as if anyone could walk in upon him and ask him any question . . . I could not see why the tippers with business did not come right in off the street and talk to him. They did not. My business was with his partners or associates, principally Samuel Spencer, but I noticed that these . . . did not go near him unless he sent for them; and then they looked alarmed and darted in like office boys. 'Nobody can answer that question except Mr Morgan,' they would tell me. Well, Mr Morgan was there; why not go in and ask him? The answer I got was a smile or a shocked look of surprise. And once, when I pressed the president of one of the Morgan banks to put to him a question we agreed deserved an answer, the banker said, 'Not on your life', and when I said, 'But why not?' he said, 'You try it yourself and see.' And I did . . . I walked into his office, and stood before him at his flat, clean, clear desk.

I stood while he examined a sheet of figures; I stood for two or three long minutes, while the whole bank seemed to stop work to watch me, and he did not look up; he was absorbed, he was sunk, in those figures. He was so alone with himself and his mind that when he did glance up he did not see me; his eyes were looking inward. He was a mathematician, you know . . . I thought, as he looked at and did not see me that day, that he was doing a sum in mental arithmetic, and when he solved it he dropped his eyes back upon his sheet of figures and I slunk out.

Somebody stopped me as I was going out through the bank and laughingly asked me what had happened.

'Nothing,' I said; 'he didn't even see me.'

'You're lucky', was the chuckling answer. 'You have to call him to wake him up. If you had said, "Mr Morgan", he would have come to. And then –'

'What would have happened then?' I asked.

'Oh,' the partner said, 'then you would have seen – an explosion.'

I believed that; it was generally believed on the Street that J. P. Morgan

*The quotations are from Steffens' *Autobiography* (Harcourt, Brace & Co., 1931).

was a dangerous man to talk to, and no doubt that made it unnecessary for him to be guarded by door men, secretaries, and stenographers. He could protect himself. I know that I came to feel, myself, what others on Wall Street felt – a vague awe of the man.

But I went through that awful circle once . . . My paper had received . . . a typewritten statement from Morgan and Company; it was some announcement about a matter of bonds that had been news for months, and the city editor called me in to read it with him. He could not make it out. It was a long, complicated statement all in one sentence, and I could not read it either. 'Take it down to Mr Morgan and ask him to read it' . . . [my boss] said, and I remember I was startled. I asked . . . him if he knew what he was asking of me: to go and put a question to the old man himself. 'Yes . . . but it has to be done.' I picked up the statement, ran down to the bank, conning the sentence, and ready for the explosion . . . walked into Morgan's office and right up to his desk. He saw me this time; he threw himself back in his chair so hard that I thought he would tip over.

'Mr Morgan,' I said as brave as I was afraid, 'what does this statement mean?' and I threw the paper down before him.

'Mean!' he exclaimed. His eyes glared, his great red nose seemed to me to flash and darken, flash and darken. Then he roared, '*Mean!* It means what it says. I wrote it myself, and it says what I mean.'

'It doesn't say anything – straight', I blazed.

He sat back there, flashing and rumbling; then he clutched the arms of his chair, and I thought he was going to leap at me. I was so scared that I defied him.

'Oh, come now, Mr Morgan . . . you may know a lot about figures and finance, but I'm a reporter, and I know as much as you do about English. And that statement isn't English.'

That was the way to treat him, I was told afterward. And it was in that case. He glared at me a moment more, the fire went out of his face, and he leaned forward over the bit of paper and said very meekly, 'What's the matter with it?'

I said I thought it would be clearer in two sentences instead of one and I read it aloud so, with a few other verbal changes.

'Yes,' he agreed, 'that is better. You fix it.'

I fixed it under his eyes, he nodded, and I, whisking it away, hurried back to the office. They told me in the bank afterward that 'J.P.' sat watching me go out of the office, then rapped for Spencer* and asked what my name was, where I came from, and said, 'Knows what he wants, and – and – gets it.'

*Samuel Spencer, a Morgan associate whom he helped make president of the Baltimore & Ohio Railroad.

One of Morgan's offices

Morgan spent much of his time on the *Corsair*, where he entertained and held important conferences. He also used the yacht to go back and forth to Cragston. He was now, at forty-nine, a very powerful figure and in relatively good physical condition. The eruption on his nose and face troubled him, however, and he did not get the physical exercise he needed – the horseback rides and the long walks were things of the past. In winter the lack of open-air life probably accounted for his frequent headaches and heavy colds; but despite his bouts of exhaustion and spells of illness, Morgan enjoyed life. He had a number of intimate friends – women as well as men; his male friends were members of the Corsair Club, which he had organized. He delighted in feminine society,

75

particularly when his lady companions were pretty and gay, and, when travelling on his yacht to eastern Mediterranean ports, he would bring back from the bazaars trayfuls of jewels and knickknacks which he distributed among them. Among his favourites was Maxine Elliott, the great beauty of the theatre. However, the playful side of Morgan was perceived by very few, for he was discretion itself. When an associate, whom he had called on the carpet for some action, protested that he was only doing what Morgan himself had been doing 'behind closed doors', Morgan replied, 'That, sir, is what doors are *for*.'

Anne Lindbergh, daughter of Dwight Morrow, a Morgan partner, gives a vivid picture of Morgan's son, J. P. Morgan, Jr, in her diary, written in the 1920s.* I quote from it here because her description of him tallies remarkably with my impression of his father: 'He greeted us at the door; a great, massive, overpowering sort of man. Shaggy eyebrows, almost a fierce gaze. A hearty and generous host – very much a host. He took great pride in it all and showed it with a kind of formal playfulness . . .' After dinner she describes listening to the men talk. 'He [Morgan] is most obstinate and determined in his remarks. Very impressive – very quick, too. I think Dr Johnson must have silenced his opponents in argument just as Mr Morgan would.'

Anne Lindbergh describes supper aboard the *Corsair*. 'We were transported very swiftly in a closed-in motor boat to the great steamer . . . We stepped out onto the steps and at the top stood Mr Morgan – great, gruff, cordial, always with his "superb" manner, large smile, large gestures, large, hearty "How do you do" – his round, very full voice, English accent.'

When, as a child, Anne Lindbergh was introduced to Morgan's father, her mother warned her not to make any remark about his nose. She was told to serve tea and, looking up at Mr Morgan, asked 'How many lumps do you want in your nose?'

Morgan occasionally revisited Hartford and during the winter of 1889 he discussed with his cousin, the Rev. Francis Goodwin, the problems of the Wadsworth Atheneum – its lack of endowment and need for more space. He suggested that they go to London and take up with his father what could be done. That spring the three men dined

*Published in 1972 as *Bring Me a Unicorn* (Harcourt, Brace, Jovanovich).

Opposite, top A French pendant jewel; *bottom* a medieval reliquary

Overleaf The Mazarin Tapestry

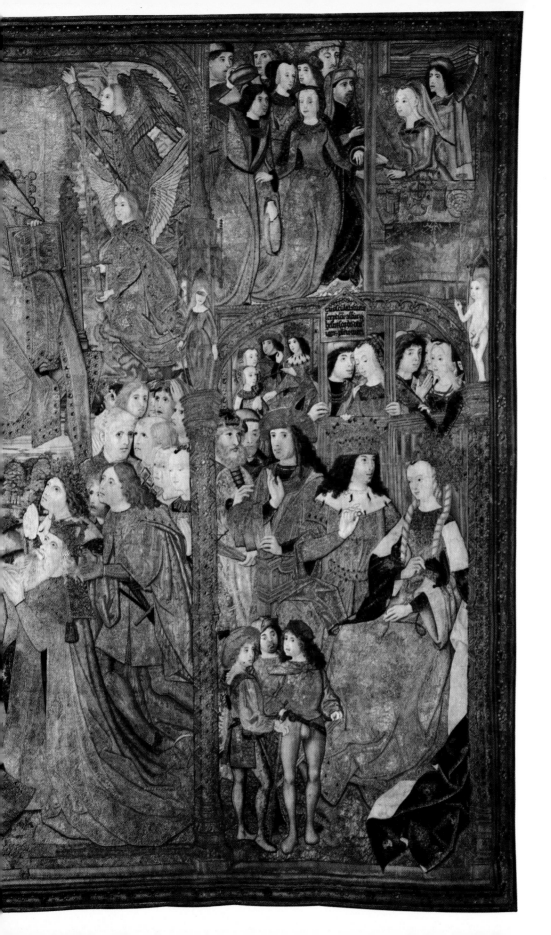

together at Princes Gate with the result that Junius Morgan contributed $100,000 to the museum; to this sum his son added $50,000. From Pierpont's collection the Wadsworth Atheneum later acquired many fine objects – particularly porcelains and antique sculpture.

In 1890 Pierpont Morgan suddenly succeeded his father as senior partner of the London house of J. S. Morgan & Company, when Junius Spencer Morgan died in an accident to his carriage on the Riviera. This came as a great shock to Pierpont, who was deeply attached to his father, with whom he had worked for so long. His mother's death four years previously at Princes Gate had also been a blow, although it had not been unexpected since she had been an invalid for many years. Three years later Anthony J. Drexel passed away, with the result that in 1895, the firm name of Drexel, Morgan & Company was changed to J. P. Morgan & Company.

In 1895 the United States' monetary condition was in peril as a consequence of the Panic of two years before. American securities arrived from Europe on every boat and they had to be paid for from a fast dwindling gold supply. At the end of January, William Curtis, Assistant Secretary of the Treasury, arrived in New York to consult August Belmont, who immediately got in touch with Morgan. As a result of their conversations J. P. Morgan & Company, in alliance with J. S. Morgan & Company of London, August Belmont & Company and the Rothschilds, agreed to consider joint action to save the credit of the U.S. Government.

At this juncture President Grover Cleveland, a strong supporter of Congressional prerogative, was relying on Congress to pass immediate legislation to solve the financial problem by authorizing a Government bond issue. Congress did nothing, and Cleveland refused to see Morgan when he arrived in Washington. Morgan was met by Daniel Lamont, Secretary of War, who said that the President had not changed his attitude. 'I have come to Washington to see the President,' Morgan said slowly, 'and I am going to stay here until I see him.' He then settled down to his solitaire – also the favourite pastime of Napoleon – and worked over 'Miss Milliken', one of his favourite games far into the small hours, arranging the cards methodically, playing almost automatically as he did when he had something on his mind. Suddenly he remembered that during the Civil War a bill had been passed permitting the Secretary of the Treasury to buy gold and pay for it with government bonds; he

81

A folio from a sixteenth-century Book of Hours

Left Princes Gate, London: Morgan inherited no. 13 and bought no. 14.
Below Morgan playing solitaire

recalled the bill as 'Section four thousand and something'. But he had no idea whether or not this Act had since been repealed.

Desperate, Cleveland finally asked Morgan to call. Only $9 million in gold coin remained in the government vaults and a draft for upwards of $10 million was about to be presented. 'If that ten million dollars is presented, you can't meet it', said Morgan. 'It will all be over by three o'clock.'

'What suggestion have you to make, Mr Morgan?' the President asked. Morgan leaned forward and talked fast; he spoke of the long-forgotten 'Section four thousand and something'. Cleveland called upon a member of his staff to look this up and was assured that the Act was still in force. From that point things moved rapidly and Morgan agreed to raise $60 million in bonds – a tremendous risk since this action meant altering normal business laws and accomplishing what the U.S. Government had found impossible. On 20 February the newspapers carried an advertisement of the bond offering, underwritten by J. P. Morgan & Company, August Belmont & Company and, in London, by N. M. Rothschild & Sons and J. S. Morgan & Company. In New York the list was kept open for twenty-two minutes and the subscription totalled $450 million.

When asked by the Finance Committee of the U.S. Senate why he had headed up this bond flotation rather than leaving it to others, Morgan replied: 'They could not do it.' It was true. Most people believed that if the United States had undertaken to underwrite and sell its own bonds, the investing public would have bought only a fraction. People lacked the confidence in their government which they had in J. Pierpont Morgan. Of course, Morgan and his associates took a big risk inasmuch as any unsold bonds would have remained indefinitely a solidly frozen asset on their books.

In 1899 Morgan entered into a transaction which, although far less important financially than the U.S. bond issue, had considerable reper-cussions. In that year the publishing firm of Harper & Brothers went into receivership. George Harvey, a prominent financier who knew Morgan and was involved in the literary world, called upon him after hearing the comment of William Dean Howells on the affair: 'It was as if I had read that the U.S. Government had failed.'

Morgan, recognizing the role Harper's played in the cultural life of the country, loaned the firm a million dollars, without hesitation, despite the unstable condition of the financial market. In due course he advanced a second million, but the loan was only partially repaid some years after his death.

Morgan made Harvey president of Harper's and, under him, the firm acquired some famous authors, including Mark Twain and Woodrow Wilson. But it was not until the 1920s that the company really prospered once more under its own steam.

VI

MORGAN AT THE APEX OF HIS CAREER –
U.S. STEEL – MORGAN SAVES THE COUNTRY
IN THE PANIC OF 1907 –
PUJO INVESTIGATION

WHEN THE war with Spain broke out, the small U.S. fleet had to be augmented by the purchase of coastwise steamers, seagoing tugs and yachts. Among the first vessels to be inspected was the *Corsair II*, a larger yacht than the first *Corsair*, which it had replaced in 1890; her beautiful mahogany was ripped out and she was converted into a gunboat. At Santiago she was victorious over the Spanish destroyers. After the war Morgan got busy on the designs of a third *Corsair*, similar to *Corsair II* with its magnificent panelled interior, but even larger. He was delighted with his splendid yacht, nearly 300 feet overall, and to a group of friends at the launching kept repeating, 'Isn't she a beauty!' Morgan was an avid yachtsman and took a keen interest in the America's Cup race. His contender, the *Columbia*, won over Sir Thomas Lipton's *Shamrock II* in 1901.

Mrs Morgan had been spending the summer abroad and, when she returned on the *Oceanic*, her husband met her on his yacht. Although sixty-four years old and weighing 210 pounds, he proceeded to climb a rope ladder from the *Corsair* to the deck of the *Oceanic*. His progress was very slow so that the people watching him turned their heads away in alarm, but he made it and, when his perspiring face appeared at the rail, he waved aside all the outstretched hands and asked, 'Where is Mrs Morgan?'

Yachting was not his only pastime. During the early 1900s Morgan devoted much time and energy to the affairs of the Metropolitan Museum of Art. Having served for some years as a trustee he was elected president in 1904. It was an honour he deserved, for not only

84

Corsair II, above, was requisitioned by the Navy.
One of Morgan's later yachts, the *Columbia, below,*
won the America's Cup.

was he knowledgeable about art but had contributed important acquisitions. When the Garland Collection of more than two thousand porcelains, which had been exhibited for many years in the museum as a loan, was sold to Henry Duveen for several hundred thousand dollars, Morgan stepped in and purchased the collection.

Morgan was now at the apex of his career and had become the acknowledged leader in Wall Street. He was concerned with most of the important industries in the country, and so it was natural that he should turn his attention to steel, which had superseded other metals for construction. The rapid development of the steel industry in the United States attracted the world's attention. Andrew Carnegie had come to dominate this field and it was his ruthless ambition to control the world market. At the head of his company was young Charles M. Schwab.

Carnegie decided to build a fleet of ore carriers, 'because', he said, 'present rates for transporting ore are so villainous.' This was big news – it sounded good to steelworkers – but to steel-iron operators, and bankers with very big investments in steel and railroads, it seemed like madness. Morgan did not like the sound of it. Schwab, in the course of a celebrated speech to a large group of businessmen of which Morgan was one, stated that cheaper steel could not be made by improved technology; it could come about only by industry-wide consolidation and specialization.

Quite possibly the success of Standard Oil sparked in many alert minds the idea of a similar merger of steel interests. Whoever the originator, it was Schwab who first advanced this idea with a conviction no other American industrialist could match. Morgan, fired by Schwab's vision, put together the Steel Corporation.

It was evident to Morgan that, to bring stabilization to the chaotic steel industry, he needed an expert to guide him, as Charles H. Coster, one of his partners, had done in the case of the railroads. He chose Judge Elbert H. Gary, 'a man of almost unendurable sanctimoniousness',* counsel for the Illinois Steel Company, and proceeded to bring together a group of steel men, known as the 'Waldorf Crowd'. Initially, he financed the Federal Steel Company, with a capitalization of $200 million. With Gary as president, Morgan's organization of the United

*Age of the Moguls by Stuart Holbrook (Doubleday & Co., 1953)

States Steel Corporation in 1901 was the most important enterprise he had ever undertaken; its capitalization of $1,400,000,000 made it the largest corporation organized up to that time. Morgan had eliminated Carnegie from big steel.

Carnegie, after he and Morgan had agreed upon $225,639,000 as the price for his steel interests, asked the financier whether he would have paid $100 million more, had that been demanded. Morgan replied, 'If you had [asked], I should have paid it.' The initial arrangement was quite informal; it was a pencilled memorandum on a scrap of paper. In due course a suitable document was prepared and signed by both parties.

Morgan's fame had spread as a result of the steel amalgamation, and more and more people here and abroad came to depend on him. It was reported that Lloyd's of London had insured his life for $20 million.

Morgan's failure to take advantage of his opportunity to reorganize the Union Pacific Railroad was one of his chief mistakes. He thought the road had no future; his archrival in this field, E. H. Harriman, on the contrary, thought it promising and in 1895, after a struggle with the interests of Kuhn, Loeb & Company (Harriman's backer and Morgan's chief competitor on Wall Street), reorganized the railroad. By 1901 the Union Pacific was considered 'the most magnificent railroad property in the world'.

Morgan and Harriman were the two great antagonists in the railroad field. One of their struggles involved control of the Burlington & Quincy, an essential line in the important transportation network west of the Missouri River. James J. Hill and Morgan wanted it because it would give the Northern Pacific an entry into Chicago; Harriman had to have it because it was a competitor for business in his Union Pacific territory.

Harriman lost the fight for control of the Burlington, and the Morgan-Hill forces breathed a heavy sigh of relief, unaware of the fact that, at the moment, Harriman was buying up the stock of the Northern Pacific, which now owned the Burlington line. In the course of this fight Northern Pacific stock went up from 112 to $149\frac{3}{4}$ in two days. No outsiders knew, with certainty, why the stock had skyrocketed, but it was the general feeling that the shares were selling well above their intrinsic value. Consequently, heavy short selling developed in the expectation that the stock would decline. Instead, Northern Pacific

Morgan, seen above on *Corsair III*, bought Carnegie *far left* out of the steel industry. The dinner celebrating the formation of the U.S. Steel Corporation was held round a table in the shape of a T-rail end section. Charles Schwab was one of the guests.

89

E. H. Harriman, characteristically in the front seat

advanced fifty points, making it impossible for the shorts to cover. On 9 May 1901 the stock sold at $1000 per share, while U.S. Steel and other quality leaders in the market fell by thirty to fifty per cent. Hill said of this speculative frenzy: 'All I can do is to compare it to an Indian "ghost dance". The Indians begin their dance and don't know why they are doing it. They whirl around until they are almost crazy. It is so when these Wall Street people get the speculation fever.'

Harriman had nearly succeeded in acquiring control of the Northern Pacific. His struggle with Morgan had become so involved and tense that the only solution was a compromise between the two warring factions. Morgan was empowered to select directors to fill vacancies on the Northern Pacific board; Harriman and a member of his associates became directors of both Northern Pacific and the Burlington line.

At the age of seventy, in the Panic of 1907, Morgan faced and over-came his supreme test. At the Triennial Episcopal Convention in Richmond, Virginia, he was handed a telegram and a member of the party said to him, 'Mr Morgan, you seem to have some bad news.' Morgan shot his eyes across the table and said nothing.

In New York the storm clouds were piling up; people were beginning to question the solvency of trust companies, which were allowed by

90

law to operate as if they were national banks, but without being subject to the strict regulations of such banks. Among those in trouble was the Knickerbocker Trust Company, and its founder, who had been a schoolfriend of Morgan's, appealed to him for help. On Tuesday, 22 October, depositors swarmed to the bank to draw out their money and that afternoon the bank failed. The news spread terror in Wall Street.

Financial panics in pre-World War I days occurred every few years. The Federal Reserve banking system was not established until 1913, and in the early 1900s the idea of a guarantee of bank deposits by the Federal Government was only a pipedream; indeed, the Government had proved itself powerless to deal with the recurrent panics. It was Pierpont Morgan who did so.

From today's viewpoint there was really little protection against financial and industrial collapse, but in those days businessmen confidently pointed to the stabilizing effects of industrial and financial concentrations. Even Morgan was unaware of the developing Panic of 1907, one of the very worst in history, despite the usual danger signals: swollen inventories, overextension of credit, inflated security prices and wild manipulation of stocks. The financial community refused to face the facts and blamed President Theodore Roosevelt, accusing him of a 'policy of hostility against all corporations and their securities, particularly railroads.'

On Wednesday, 23 October, Morgan was suffering from one of his heavy colds and could not be reached until his doctor, after an hour's heroic work, got him dressed and down to breakfast. Had the doctor failed, the country would have gone down the drain. In one of the worst days of the country's economic history, the Westinghouse Company failed and the Pittsburgh Stock Exchange suspended dealings. Morgan invited the presidents of the trust companies to his office as one bank after another was threatened. One of the worst trouble spots was the Trust Company of America, which Morgan saved that day by supplying the necessary cash.

Thursday and Friday were worse. On Thursday morning Morgan drove downtown in a brougham drawn by a white horse; along the way pedestrians, cabbies and policemen recognized him and shouted, 'There goes the Old Man!' or 'There goes the Big Chief!' The storm centre was now the Stock Exchange, where prices had collapsed. R. H. Thomas, the president of the Exchange, called at 23 Wall Street in desperation

Morgan the stork delivers newborn
confidence to an expectant Wall
Street.

Belle da Costa Greene

and, according to Herbert Satterlee, Morgan's son-in-law, said, 'Mr Morgan, we will have to close the Stock Exchange.' *'What?'* said Morgan, turning sharply. 'It must not close one moment before that hour [three o'clock] today!', emphasizing each word by keeping time with the right hand, the middle finger pointing straight at Mr Thomas. Summoning instantly the presidents of all the national banks in the neighbourhood, Morgan raised $25 million within a matter of minutes. The Exchange remained open.

The next day $13 million did the trick, but George W. Perkins, a Morgan partner, observed: 'There was not a ray of hope in the situation.' Again Morgan called together the bank presidents, this time at the office of the Clearing House. Satterlee writes:

> Anyone who saw Mr Morgan going from the Clearing House back to his office that day will never forget the picture. With his coat unbuttoned and flying open, a piece of paper clutched tightly in his right hand, he walked fast down Nassau Street, his flat-topped derby set firmly down on his head; his eyes fixed straight ahead. He was the embodiment of power and purpose.

Night after night conferences took place in the Morgan Library; Morgan would sit in a red-plush armchair by the fire in the West Room. Young Miss Belle Greene, his trusted librarian, acted as messenger and brought him messages from the assembled bankers in the East Room, interrupting his solitaire. More than once during this long session, which lasted until midnight, one of the bankers was deputed to present a plan to Morgan. He would look up, listen attentively and then shake his head, saying, 'No, that will not work', and return to his cards without further comment. After this had happened two or three times, Miss Greene asked Morgan, 'Why don't you tell them what to do?' and he answered: 'I don't know what to do myself, but sometime, someone will come in with a plan that I know *will* work; and then I will tell them what to do.' Eventually, a plan to issue Clearing House certificates was presented. Morgan did not like the idea but said, nevertheless, 'This will work', and approved it.

At last the dreadful week came to an end. Theodore Roosevelt, who had so often berated 'malefactors of great wealth', and who had said of Morgan, 'He seems to regard me as a rival operator', gave out a confident statement praising 'those influential and splendid business-men . . . who have acted with such wisdom and public spirit.' The worst seemed to be over, but the crisis continued and there were two further periods of acute danger: one when the City of New York needed $30 million at once to pay off short-term obligations; another over the weekend of 2 and 3 November when Moore & Schley, important brokers, faced collapse.

Late on Saturday, 2 November, the battle against the panic reached its climax; Morgan once more received the bank presidents in the Library. It was an exhausting evening following two weeks of unrelieved tension; everyone felt at the end of his tether. Benjamin Strong, of the Bankers Trust Company, sitting next to James Stillman of the National City Bank, dozed off to sleep, and the latter asked him when he had last been to bed. 'Thursday night' was the reply. At last Strong was called to make his report to Morgan. Then, feeling that he had the right to go home, he went to the front door. It had been locked by Morgan.

The assembled bankers' pockets were empty, and they could see no possibility of putting up another $25 million to save the situation. Finally, Morgan walked into the room where they were sitting; his bulk was imposing and, with his swollen and vivid nose, he presented a terrifying appearance. As Edward Steichen observed, 'Meeting his black eyes was like confronting the headlights of an express train bearing down on you.' He had with him a document providing that each trust company, according to its resources, would put up its share of the financial support that was required. 'There you are, gentlemen,' he said.

No one stepped forward.

Morgan put his hand on the shoulder of Edward King, leader of the group. 'There's the place, King, and here's the pen.'

King signed; they all signed. Morgan had carried the day; it was quarter to five in the morning and the panic was over. To the extent one man could exercise the function of a central banking system, Morgan had done it – he had been a one-man Federal Deposit Insurance Corporation.

When a banker had said to him during the panic, 'I am very disturbed, I am below my legal reserve', Morgan replied, 'You ought to be ashamed of yourself. What is your reserve for at a time like this except to use?' And so he bludgeoned others into displaying the courage that was his supreme contribution.

In his biography of Henry P. Davison, Thomas W. Lamont relates an incident which occurred on the first day, in 1911, that Davison went

The Steichen camera portrait of Morgan

to work as a Morgan partner. The Carnegie Trust Company was in trouble and runs had started on other banks in poor neighbourhoods in upper Manhattan. Representatives of those banks called on Lamont and William H. Porter, another partner, to see if Morgan & Company would help in the emergency. Porter was doubtful and telephoned Morgan at the Library to get his advice. Whereupon, according to Lamont, Morgan, learning that the two banks had some thirty thousand depositors, mostly poor, said:

> Well, some way *must* be found to help those poor people. We mustn't let them lose all they have in the world. Suppose that, at most, we were to guarantee these deposits in full. You say the total is only six million dollars? That means that the firm can't lose more than six million dollars, doesn't it?

Morgan & Company thereupon backed the banks and, because of the prestige of the firm, restored confidence, suffering a loss of only $190,000.

Morgan had a very strong sense of fiduciary responsibility. In 1905 he purchased, as agent for the Erie Railroad without commission, a controlling interest in a small line known as the Cincinnati, Hamilton & Dayton and found that the figures that had been shown to him did not reveal the real financial condition of the railroad, which was in a very bad way. One of Morgan's partners observed: 'It was incredible to him that anyone should show him false figures.' Morgan immediately bought back the line from the Erie at the same price that Erie had paid for it – $12 million – and put it into receivership at what proved to be a virtually total loss to Morgan & Company.

This complicated, gruff man combined humility with arrogance. In London he became so exercised over his employees who, in the class-conscious British fashion, bowed to him, that he ordered them to desist on pain of dismissal. Yet he *had* to have his way; when he could not get a friend of his into the Union Club, he proceeded to build his own, which was known as the Metropolitan Club.

Morgan was a tycoon of his period, and he thought of industry not in terms of its thousands of workers – of human beings – but in terms of the investors who supported it and of the directors whose duty it was to protect and enrich the investors. For those directors his standards were high; they must be honest and, preferably, gentlemen. In fact, he would have liked to see the United States run by gentlemen, and it did not occur to him that these gentlemen might be insulated from their

Mrs Morgan, and Mr Morgan with
a granddaughter in 1902

fellow men and might run things in a way most comfortable to themselves. After all, he would observe, the politicians liked to run things to
their advantage. So, although loyal to his country and its Government,
his ideas were kingly, as was his conduct of life; the idea of democracy
evaded him.*

Morgan shared the view of women held by many of his contemporaries; he did not see much use in educating them, nor did he consider them responsible in money matters. In his will the money allotted
to his daughters was left in trust, while to his male heirs he willed
property outright.

He believed that children should be kept in their place, yet he enjoyed
their company. Although he did not play their games nor read aloud
to them, he liked to have children playing around as he consumed his
huge breakfasts. He was particularly fond of his grandchild, Mabel
Satterlee, and would reach out his hand and hold hers. He used to

*This paragraph is a paraphrase of one in Frederick Lewis Allen's *The Great Pierpont Morgan*
(Harper & Brothers, 1949).

scatter lumps of sugar under the table so that she would be happy and quiet as he talked business to his partners before going to the office.

Morgan was a father symbol to his young; reserved but generous and usually ready for a joke: when a child lost a tooth, he would wrap it carefully and make out that he intended to have it mounted for his art collection.

After the experience of 1907 Morgan's retirement from business was progressive. He was often to be seen in his suite at a continental Grand Hotel seated at a card table reaching for a silver box containing two packs of cards. He dressed formally, with a wing collar, Ascot tie and white waistcoat; beside him sat Chun, his Pekingese dog.

Or he would be found in London, entering a Bond Street gallery, wearing a silk hat and overcoat with a velvet collar and carrying a gold-headed cane. There, a diverse assortment of objets d'art and a Flemish tapestry would be set out for his inspection. 'How much for the stack?' Morgan asked. The dealer named a sum in six figures, to which Morgan replied, 'Right!' and departed. Or he would be seen at Duveen's, where James Henry Duveen would produce a photograph, and say, 'This is a picture of the vases about which I wrote you.' Morgan pounced on the photo, 'How much?' '£22,000.' 'Much too dear', replied Morgan as he walked out.

Or he would be at home in the Library with Belle Greene and a pile of letters the size of which appalled her. Morgan observed that he had found that, if you leave letters alone long enough, they 'die out'. After a while he would ask Miss Greene to read aloud the story of Jonah and the whale from the Bible. When she inquired whether he really believed it, he said that he did, implicitly; that when the time came that he could not accept every word in the Bible, he would believe none of it. At times he would sit motionless in his chair, the cigar ashes dropping on his waistcoat as the minutes ticked by and he would not move; his eyes were far away as he sat lost in thought.

During the Pujo Senatorial investigation in 1912 into monopolies, Samuel Untermyer, the committee's counsel, questioned Morgan relentlessly about his overriding influence in national finance. The Morgan interests held: 118 directorships in 34 banks or trust companies; 30 directorships in 10 insurance companies; 105 directorships

98

Morgan caricatured after the Pujo
investigation: *left* as the Trust King;
below 'powerless'!

in 32 transportation companies; 63 directorships in 24 producing and trading corporations; and 25 directorships in 12 public utility corporations; making a total of 341 directorships in 112 corporations. The combined corporations had resources of over $22,000 million, and of the 341 directorships Morgan's partners held 72.

At the close of its report the Pujo Committee included these words: 'The acts of this inner group . . . have . . . been more destructive of competition than anything accomplished by the trusts.'

Questioned about his alleged control of the banks, Morgan insisted that the presence of Morgan partners on the boards of other banking institutions did not mean control, that the influence which men exercised depended not on diagrams of 'control' but upon their personal stature. Untermyer had asked him: 'Is not commercial credit based primarily on money or property?' 'No, sir,' answered Morgan, 'the first thing is character.' 'Before money or property?' 'Before anything else. Money cannot buy it . . . because a man I do not trust could not get money from me on all the bonds in Christendom.'

Shortly after the Pujo affair he received George Harvey, editor of *Harper's Weekly*, who had for some time been a strong backer of the Democrat, Woodrow Wilson, although he turned against him later. In the course of their talk Harvey quoted the lines, 'Who never to himself hath said, "This is my own, my native land." ' Morgan, the staunch Republican, sat still for half a minute, then said slowly to Harvey, 'When you see Mr Wilson, tell him from me that if there should ever come a time when he thinks any influence or resources I may have can be used for my country, they are wholly at his disposal.' Morgan had faith in his country and once said, 'Never sell America short.'

His last years brought many discouragements; the distrust of great wealth grew, and under Theodore Roosevelt more and more laws were passed regulating business. In 1911 the Federal Government brought suit against Morgan's creation – the U.S. Steel Corporation – for combination in restraint of trade, a suit which the corporation subsequently won. 'Well, it has come to this!' Morgan exclaimed sadly to his son-in-law, Herbert Satterlee.

VII

HOW MORGAN BUILT UP HIS COLLECTION –
THE PRINCES GATE PERIOD

W HILE OTHER New York millionaires built themselves ostentatious replicas of French châteaux or Renaissance palazzi, Morgan was content to live in his comfortable inconspicuous brownstone on Murray Hill. And he refused to spend his summers in fashionable Newport, preferring his solid and rather stolid country house Cragston on the Hudson. Morgan set his own style and, when he started at a late age seriously to build up his art collection, he did so with princely assurance. Many art dealers, disappointed because Morgan did not buy their wares, consoled themselves by calling him a vulgar wholesaler. As Francis Henry Taylor wrote: 'He was accused of not looking at an object when, in reality, he was looking into the eye of the man who was trying to sell it to him.'

As a child in Switzerland, Morgan had collected fragments of stained glass which he found outside churches and, over the next few decades, he picked up various objets d'art, including some typically mediocre pictures by the French salon artists of the 1880s.

In the Azores he had lived close to the Portuguese fisherfolk and developed a liking for maritime life and yachting that lasted throughout his life. His letters home were full of detailed descriptions of trinkets and souvenirs; they reveal his intensity of observation and love of craftsmanship. Although in the course of time Morgan surrounded himself with great masterpieces of painting and although he had a very perceptive eye, he tended to be more interested in the artifact than in the image. Upon Morgan's death the *Burlington Magazine* expressed the opinion:

> His feeling for works of art was the outcome rather of a romantic and historical feeling for the splendor of past ages than a strictly aesthetic one. What he recognized in an object was primarily its importance, the part it had played in the evolution of civilization.

101

A late twelfth-century English representation of incidents from the life of David

Morgan, as a collector, bore a resemblance to the Medicis and the great Papal collectors; they had in common a love of goldwork, of jewels and of all sorts of precious things.

An early photo of the drawing room of the New York house shows many pictures on the walls, but no significant art purchases are recorded before the middle 1880s. A catalogue of Morgan books dated 1883 reveals only a good reading library, a number of useful art books, sets of standard authors and a few rare autographs. However, in time, his library became important. This evaluation of it appeared in Seymour de Ricci's *Census*:

> [It has] the most extensive and the most beautifully selected series of manuscripts existing on the American Continent, and it may truthfully claim to be superior in general quality to all but three or four of the greatest libraries in the Old World.

By the middle nineties Morgan's collecting for the library was in full swing, ranging from the Gutenberg Bible on vellum to the original manuscript of Keat's *Endymion*. His biggest coup was the purchase of the collection of Richard Bennett of Manchester; among the incunabula were thirty-two Caxtons. The collection cost Morgan $700,000 and was the largest purchase ever made for the library.

In *Lines of Memory* George S. Hellman wrote: 'Whether or not the Morgan Library or the Huntington is the foremost collection of books in the world is a moot question; but concerning original manuscripts there can be no dispute.'*

Bishop William Lawrence made this comment on Morgan's pertinacity:

> The persistency with which he could follow up what really interested him was remarkable. I remember his telling me how he obtained the Byron manuscripts. 'I was told,' he said, 'in London, that the Byron manuscripts were in the possession of a lady, a relative of Byron, in Greece. Libraries in England were after them. I wanted them. I therefore, through the advice of an expert, engaged a man, gave him a letter of credit and told him to go to Greece and live [there] until he had gotten those manuscripts. Every once in a while, during several years, a volume would come which the relative had been willing to sell, until the whole was complete.'

*Hellman forgot about the British Museum!

103

In the nineteenth century the great dynastic fortunes were few in New York. Town houses were quite modest; Murray Hill was a pleasant residential village where the residents epitomized a life of bourgeois luxury. Neither new ideas nor new faces were welcomed. In the middle decades upper-class citizens possessed only moderate wealth, largely derived from increase in real estate values; the proceeds were usually reinvested in growing Manhattan or used for the opening of the West. So there was little money in the second half of the century for art collecting as it was practised abroad.

Morgan's first passion as a serious collector was for rare books and manuscripts, and it was only when he had reached his sixties and inherited his father's fortune that he started to buy art objects on a grand scale. He began late partly out of deference to his father, with whom he did not wish to compete, although the latter collected on quite a modest scale. Following his father's death in 1890, Morgan took the plunge and spent more than half his fortune on works of art. One did not have the museum feeling in viewing Mr Morgan's treasures; his houses were homes enriched by beautiful things; they were not buildings erected for display.

His collection was diverse. As one views the objects along with those acquired by other collectors, one can often recognize Morgan pieces, which are usually distinguishable by their bright colours and by a certain grandeur. But not always; his countless fine miniatures and small objects – carved ivories, champlevé enamels – testify to his delight in the delicate and the minute.

Morgan's taste was traditional – sometimes sentimental; he always kept on the window sill at Princes Gate the ordinary China pug dogs collected by his mother. Another instance of his sentimental approach occurred when the voluble rare-book dealer, George S. Hellman, brought to him manuscripts belonging to S. W. Wakeman, a wealthy New Yorker. Morgan did not have the time to look at them before going abroad; consequently, Wakeman withdrew his offer to sell, but Hellman kept one manuscript – a poem by Longfellow. Upon Morgan's return from Europe, Hellman saw him and explained the situation, urging Morgan to make an offer for the whole collection. 'Here's one of the poems and, if you will excuse me for being personal, whenever I read it, I think of your grandchildren.'

'What's that?' said Morgan in his quick, incisive way. He was not

The incipit page of *De Spiritu Sancto*

INCIPIT PRAEFATIO S HIERO
NYMI IN LIBRO S DIDYMI
GRAECI MONACHI ALEXAN
DRINI DE SPIRITV SANCTO.

Dum in babilone uersarer et pur
purate meretricis essem colonus et
iure qui nium uiuerem adiudicali
quid garrire de spiritu sancto et

used to having his private sentiments brought into a business discussion.

Hellman then showed the poem to Morgan, who put on his spectacles
and read:

> Between the dark and the daylight,
> When the night is beginning to lower,
> Comes a pause in the day's occupations,
> That is known as the Children's Hour.

When Morgan finished reading this, he hit the table with his fist. 'I'll
take the collection!' he exclaimed. (Morgan's grandchildren would romp
around the library and were among the very few who held him in no
awe.)

Hellman writes:

> He had that forward looking imagination which enabled him to
> visualize the collector's sphere far in advance, so that those items ac-
> quired by him – whether paintings by great masters, marvelous Chinese
> porcelains, or manuscripts of Keats or Burns that might seem to have
> been purchased at high prices at the time – proved to be bargains long
> before Mr Morgan's years were ended. It was the same kind of imagination
> which, functioning in the world of business, qualified him to understand
> the potentialities of an industry while still in its infancy.

Hellman later brought to Morgan a small Vermeer painting. 'Who's
Vermeer?' asked Morgan (not a surprising response since, at the time,
there were only four paintings by Vermeer in the United States). The
dealer told Morgan some facts about the Dutch painter, adding that his
work was almost unobtainable by private collectors.

Then Morgan looked at the picture more closely and asked the price.
It was $100,000. 'I'll take it', said Morgan. Hellman commented: 'The
whole affair took only a few moments and here was a collector who
was willing to pay this large sum for a picture by an artist of whose
existence he had not been aware a quarter of an hour earlier. No one
but Mr Morgan could have done this.'

The basic elements of the Morgan collecting pattern were instant
decisions and no haggling. Satterlee tells about Morgan's purchase of a
Spanish painting, a *Portrait of a Child*, which was submitted to him, in
London, as a Velasquez:

107

The Nuremberg Ship

Left A champlevé enamel plaque from a portable altar, showing the Nativity, attributed to Wilbert of Aix-la-Chapelle
Below left A bishop from a twelfth- or thirteenth-century English set of ivory chessmen
Below The enamelled lid of a watch made in Paris *c.* 1650

Champlevé enamel decoration on the back of what is thought to be
a portable altar, possibly Danish, from the early twelfth century

At the time this picture was shown him he told the dealer to leave it
until he could study it and consider the matter. This was quite according
to his custom. The dealer left it on a chair at Princes Gate. There was no
documentary evidence that went with it, but it was a charming little
picture, painted undoubtedly in Velasquez's time . . . Of course, when a
picture like that was left for Mr Morgan to consider, it was not hidden.
The other dealers who came saw it in turn. One of them might say, 'Oh,
I know where that came from. I was offered that a year ago at such-and-
such a price. It is not an original.' Another would remark: 'That picture
was sold at Christie's ten years ago, but its authenticity is in question. I
hope, Mr Morgan, that you have not bought it as an original, nor paid
much for it as a picture.' And so on. Mr Morgan always listened to it all
without comment. Before he made up his mind whether he wanted the
picture or not he would get someone from the Berlin Museum who happened to be in London, or an expert connected with one of the great
London public galleries, to stop in and look at the picture. If it was not
documented and the preponderance of the best opinion was against it, he
rejected it.

In the case of this picture of the Spanish child, when the dealer came
back and said, 'Well, Mr Morgan, what do you think?' he answered, 'You
cannot prove the picture is Velasquez's, and I feel quite sure it is not.'

109

'All right', said the dealer. 'I will take it away.' And he started to pick it up.

'No', said Mr Morgan. 'Leave it right where it is. No matter who painted it, I have become very fond of it and I am going to keep it.'

Morgan had an extraordinary eye for art (he was talented, too, as a sketcher) and, although his acquisitions were vast, he never forgot any item he had purchased.

A genuine Cosway snuffbox in gold and horn, with a miniature of the Marchioness of Donegal

Dr George C. Williamson, 'that Nestor of all art connoisseurs', became one of Morgan's firmest friends. They first met when Williamson, then unknown to Morgan, came to Princes Gate in about 1906 to look at the works of art. He was shown into the house by the butler, who remained with him as he examined, with wonder, the delicate master-pieces there. He was staring at the Fauconberg miniature, framed in diamonds. Without looking around, he said:

'May I take this to the window to look at it more closely?'

'Do what you like', came a gruff bark in his ear.

Williamson spun around; there was the emperor of finance himself. A grim smile was on his face as he observed the doctor's amazement.

'Know who I am, eh? So you are the man who never makes a mistake!'

110

'I – I've never said that', stammered the connoisseur.

'You *admit* to mistakes, then?'

'A good few. But I've owned up every time I found myself in the wrong.'

Morgan gave a hoot of laughter and said, 'I've made many enough in my own affairs. Have you found any among these? That Fauconberg miniature, for instance?'

'Well – er – ', stammered the unhappy doctor. 'I'm afraid you have been imposed upon here.'

'How?'

'I see that on the back of the old gold case Cosway's name is engraved. It is not by Cosway at all!'

Morgan's eyebrows shot up into his hair.

'You seem pretty sure!'

'Yes, Mr Morgan.' He added that the miniature was by Jean and stood twisting the Jean in his hand, feeling very uncomfortable.

There was a long silence; at last Morgan spoke.

'Now come and have some lunch.'

'I've been looking for a mind like yours!' he barked. 'I would like you to make catalogues of my collections so that . . . students can work as though they had the originals in front of them . . . I want fine colour plates, and if colour blocks won't do, then the work will have to be done by hand. Bring together the best artists you can find . . . It will be a kind of human photography!'

Swept away by Morgan's extraordinary personality and enthusiasm, Williamson felt that nothing was impossible. When he mentioned the almost fantastic cost of the project, Morgan produced a cheque book and banged it on the table.

'*Money?* I don't care about the cost! You will have to make journeys to Europe, to America and the East – fifty journeys. What does that matter? . . . Understand me, Williamson, when I say that the job will take years.'

From that moment on the two men became intimates. In his joy at having found unbiased honesty Morgan revealed the human side to his character which he hid from most of his friends. At once the doctor organized his little army of some fifty artists.*

*Adapted from *Secrets of an Art Dealer* by James Henry Duveen (E. P. Dutton, 1938).

The Duchess of Devonshire by Thomas Gainsborough

In Morgan's London house hung Gainsborough's *Duchess of Devonshire*. It had been displayed to the admiring crowds at Agnew's gallery in London many years before in 1876. On the morning of 26 May in that year the gallery caretaker found to his horror that the picture had been taken out of its frame during the night and stolen. The theft, described by William Agnew as a 'public outrage more than a private calamity', brought the picture world-wide fame. Worth was the name of the thief; he found he had a white elephant on his hands and took the picture to Chicago.

A few months after the theft a letter was received by Agnew's, reading:

> We beg to inform you of the safe arrival of your picture in America and enclose a small portion of it to satisfy you that we are the bona fide holders of your picture . . . There being no extradition between this country and England at present, we can treat you with impunity. This communication must be strictly confidential . . . on the first intimation of any police interference, we will immediately destroy the picture . . . We want $15,000 in gold . . . Insert an advertisement in the London *Times*, if you will treat on these terms, viz. *New York* letter received, etc.

Letters and cables were exchanged and Scotland Yard was, of course, notified; in August of 1877 the negotiations petered out. Over the next two decades the *Duchess* was 'discovered' eleven times. Finally, in 1899, Morland Agnew received some encouraging news from the Pinkerton Detective Agency in the United States and set sail immediately. He met Pinkerton at the Auditorium Hotel in Chicago and, in his words:

> As the hour approached when the picture would be returned I noticed Mr Pinkerton became more and more nervous than I myself . . . By and by there came a knock at the door . . . an adult messenger was standing in the doorway, carrying a brown paper roll in his arm. The messenger handed me the roll in silence and, as if he had been charged with the most commonplace message in the world, turned on his heel and left the room.

It was the *Duchess.*

On arrival in London Morland Agnew wrote: 'Papers full of reports of the finding of the *Duchess*. Make rather much use of my name . . . am getting sick of the *Duchess*.' In a few days the music halls were ringing with songs about this famous lady and Duchess of Devonshire hats became a raging fashion.* One day, the butler told Morgan that a representative of Messrs Agnew had called and said that he had the picture with him. 'Where is he? I want to see him', said Morgan. 'He was just going to sail for home and is gone.' Morgan said:

*From *Agnew's – 1817–1967* (privately printed, 1967)

113

The paintings are, from the left: *Lady Betty Delmé and Her Children*, *Mrs Tennant* (by Gainsborough), *Mrs Scott Jackson* and *The Godsall Children* (called *The Setting Sun* by Hoppner). Three of these hung in Morgan's Princes Gate dining-room.

I was determined to have that picture and I took the next ship to England. My ship was faster than his. He arrived in London on Saturday, I on Sunday. I sent word to one of the firm that I must see him on Monday morning. . . . He came to Prince's Gate and I said, 'You have the *Duchess of Devonshire*.' 'Yes', he replied. 'You remember that my father, on the afternoon before that picture was stolen, was about to buy it and was going to make his decision that next morning. He wanted it. What my father wanted, I want, and I must have the *Duchess*,' 'Very good', said the dealer. 'What is the price?' I asked. 'That is for you to say, Mr Morgan.' 'No, whatever price your firm thinks is fair, I pay.'

Asked later what the *Duchess* had cost him, Morgan said, 'Nobody will ever know. If the truth came out, I might be considered a candidate for the lunatic asylum.' The *Duchess of Devonshire* was hung in Princes Gate.

Above A *carnet de bal* of gold and enamels by Joseph Etienne Blerzy of Paris, *c.* 1782. The miniature is after Boucher.
Right The *Ange de Lude*, once a weather vane

Bishop Lawrence, a great friend of Morgan, describes Princes Gate:

Every smallest ornament or richest picture had the hallmark of his individuality. When he came away from the library, the library seemed empty; however rich the trappings, they took their proper place, merely as trappings of the man. It was this that made his manner of life seem princely. . . .

I doubt whether there has ever been a private dwelling house so filled with works of the richest art. As one entered the front door, he was still in a conventional London house, until passing along three or four yards, his eye turned and looked through the door on the left into the dining-room – in size an ample city dining-room, but in glory of color such as few other domestic dining-rooms ever enjoyed. The visitor was amazed and thrilled at the pictures: Sir Joshua Reynolds' masterpiece, *Madame Delmé and Children*, a great full-length portrait of a lady by Gainsborough, another [of *Mrs Scott Jackson*] by Romney. One's eye seemed to pierce the wall into the outer world through the landscapes of Constable [*The White Horse*] and Hobbema. Behind Mr Morgan's chair at the end of the table hung a lovely Hoppner of three children [*The Godsall Children*], a beautiful boy

115

The Annunciation by Hans Memling

standing in the center, full of grace. Why did Mr Morgan have this picture behind him? If you would sit in his chair, which faced the front of the house with the two windows looking out upon the hedge and trees of Hyde Park, you would discover between these two windows a narrow mirror, which enabled Mr Morgan to have before him always the reflected portrait of the figure of the boy. As one passed through the hall, each picture was a gem. In the center of the hall, where the dividing wall used to stand, was a graceful bronze figure, turning at will upon its base, once the weather vane of the Sainte Chapelle [*Ange de Lude*, now in the Frick collection]; near it a stone figure from the Duomo of Florence; cabinets standing about with reliquaries, statuettes and other figures.

In his biography of Morgan, Frederick Lewis Allen wrote:

Morgan was a man who did not do things by halves. [You may remember that in his earliest days in business, when he bought coffee in New Orleans, he bought the whole shipload.] Once he became enamored of collecting, he went at it in the same overwhelming way in which he went at a business reorganization. As the *Burlington* magazine said of him after his death, 'Having become the greatest financier of his age, he determined to be the greatest collector.' When Morgan decided to build a yacht, he wanted it to be the biggest one. When he bred collies, he wanted them to win the best blue ribbons. He was the sort of man who, when he takes up a sport, at once dreams of becoming the champion. When he went into collecting, nothing would satisfy him but the complete conquest of the marts of beauty – annihilating competition, taking his various objectives by frontal assault.

So completely did this ambition occupy him that, as the *Burlington* said, he 'had little leisure left for contemplation.'

It may be that the editorial in the *Burlington Magazine* was the soundest witness to Morgan the collector:

. . . In the world of art quite as much as in the world of finance, Mr Morgan was above everything a man of action. His successful raids upon the private collections of Europe were organized and carried out with the rapid decisive energy of a great general. He believed in military methods; he regarded rapidity and irrevocability of decision as more important than accuracy of judgment; he considered discipline more effective than a nice discrimination. And in spite of many instances of failure it would be rash to say that for the end he had in view his choice of means was a wrong one.

117

Left A gold box decorated in enamel, with two miniatures painted in gouache (an acrobatic performance on the cover; a puppet show on the base), by Joseph Etienne Blerzy, *c.* 1778
Below Two eighteenth-century French snuffboxes of gold and enamel set with precious stones. The miniature on the left is of Alexander I of Russia, and on the right possibly of the Princesse de Lamballe.

When Morgan had acquired the best in any field, he quit. Mrs Burns, his sister, said after Morgan's arrival in Naples: 'Pierpont, aren't you going to see a dealer in Greek antiquities?'

'No,' he replied.

'But,' she said, 'you have always gone there and bought . . .'

Morgan again said no. 'I have done with Greek antiquities; I am at the Egyptian.' His active mind moved from one interest to another – in his collection were the best miniatures, the best in English portraits and landscapes, the richest in Limoges and porcelains and bronzes, etc.

118

Triton Blowing His Trumpet, attributed to Lorenzi

The Toilet by Gerard Terborch

Nicolaes Ruts by Rembrandt

He made it a practice to collect other men's collections. 'What's the use of bothering about one little piece?' he would say. His methods seemed brusque: 'I've heard enough', he would tell a dealer. 'I'll take it for what you paid, plus ten per cent.* What did you pay?' Morgan was accused of driving prices up and of buying fakes and passing them off on the Metropolitan Museum. Actually, prices for certain types of art objects did increase threefold during the twenty years of his intensive buying. He used to say, 'No price is too high for an object of unquestioned beauty and known authenticity.' And he did acquire some fakes, which is understandable in view of the scale of his purchases. Nevertheless, few collectors have been able to combine quality with quantity in so many fields of art. He looked for the masterpieces in paintings, furniture, bronzes, enamels, porcelains, ivories, miniatures, tapestries, armour and antiquities. Like many men built on a grand scale, he delighted in small objects.

Morgan had an eye for quality and value. Joseph Duveen had his first brush with him in the 1890s. Duveen had assembled a collection of thirty miniatures, among which six were rare and the rest undistinguished. Morgan glanced at them and asked the price for the lot. When Duveen named a figure, the great collector put the six best in his pocket and figured six-thirtieths of the asking price and announced what his purchase had cost. 'You're only a boy, Joe,' his uncle Henry chortled. 'It takes a man to deal with Morgan.' Another story, perhaps apocryphal, is that when Morgan purchased some early Christian silver plates which had been dug up in Cyprus, a dealer told him they were fakes, recently made by a Neapolitan silversmith. Without hesitation Morgan replied: 'Anything else this gentleman created I should be interested in purchasing.' The plates were genuine and are now in the Metropolitan.

In the spring of 1900 Morgan telephoned Charles McKim, the leading architect of the time, and told him that he wished to have built a library next to his house, replacing the stable. McKim agreed to do so and, as the plans were being completed in 1902 said: 'I would like to build it after the manner of the Greeks, whose works have lasted through the ages. But to do so will be very expensive, and the results will not be apparent.'

'Explain', Mr Morgan demanded.

*Ten per cent, according to Roger Fry; fifteen per cent, according to others.

122

The Swing by Hubert Robert

'When I have been in Athens,' McKim continued, 'I have tried to insert the blade of my knife between the stones of the Erectheum, and have been unable to do it. I would like to follow their example, but it would cost a small fortune, and no one would see where the additional money went.'

'How much extra?' Morgan asked.

'$50,000', McKim replied.

'Go ahead.'

The library was a triumph of McKim's art and the cost was not lessened by the pinkish-white marble, each block polished to meet exactly, without mortar, in the Greek manner.

An important contemporary architect, when recently asked by the author of this book what building he considered the most beautiful in the world, chose the Morgan Library.

At the time the library was being constructed a workman on the job wrote this doggerel, which became popular:

> My name is Morgan
> But it ain't J. P.
> There's no bank on Wall Street
> That belongs to me.
> Forget your champagne appetite
> The best you'll get is beer tonight.
> My name is Morgan
> But it ain't J. P.

When Morgan became its president, in 1904, the Metropolitan Museum of Art was a relatively small enterprise, operating on an annual budget of $185,000. By the time Morgan died in 1913 this expense had increased to $363,000. Although the city contributed, there were deficits to be met and they were picked up by millionaires Morgan had put on the board, men like Henry Clay Frick, George F. Baker and Edward S. Harkness.

Shortly after Morgan had assumed the presidency, the post of director of the Metropolitan fell vacant and Sir Caspar Purdon Clarke, the director of the South Kensington Museum (now the Victoria and Albert Museum) of London, was chosen for it. His departure from London gave rise to a famous anecdote. The secretary of the South Kensington had entered bids for some Chinese porcelains and some

125

A fourteenth-century statuette of the Visitation

Morgan to John Bull: 'What else have you for sale?'

Morgan's Library

tapestries which were to be auctioned. Upon his return from a short trip he inquired about the porcelains and was told by an aide that Mr Morgan had bought them. The secretary then asked about the tapestries and the answer came, 'He got them, too.' 'Good God!' the secretary exclaimed, 'I must talk to Sir Purdon.' 'Sorry, sir,' the aide replied, 'Mr Morgan bought him, also.'

The New York climate affected Sir Purdon Clarke's health and this necessitated his taking a year's leave of absence. During this period Edward Robinson was appointed assistant director. At the same time Morgan, who pioneered the recruitment of trained museum personnel, sought to hire another Englishman whose tenure would be briefer than Purdon Clarke's, but more stormy. Roger Fry was a prickly intellectual snob, without tact and with a dislike for Americans and a contempt for great wealth which, nevertheless, fascinated him. He observed: 'Like all other Europeanized people here we make signals to one another in this weltering waste of the American people. It is strange what an invariable bond of sympathy this instinctive hatred of America, as it exists today, is.' However, he admitted: 'I meet, pretty often, men of the finest culture and the frankest openness and genuineness – men like Mark Twain . . . really fine, generous and liberal-minded.' Fry vacillated from warm admiration of the United States to bewilderment and denunciation.

Fry, who began his career as a scientist, was recognized as one of the leading art critics of the time, perhaps the foremost; his credentials were nearly as impressive as Bernard Berenson's. His early impressions of Morgan were hardly reassuring; he wrote his wife that he had found him 'the most repulsively ugly man – with a great strawberry nose'; yet he was obviously 'a very remarkable and powerful man'. Fry's worst insult to Morgan was his remark: 'A crude historical imagination was the only flaw in his otherwise perfect insensibility toward art.'

Roger Fry's first visit to America in 1905 was short and crowded with conflicting impressions; he found himself more of a celebrity in New York than in London. He stayed with Morgan and was astonished by the luxury of American millionaires; he travelled in Morgan's private railroad car, which had a fire lit when it was cold and snowing outside. In his words, 'It was fitted up like a private house in the grandest style.'* Following one of these trips Fry attended a lunch in

*Roger Fry: A Biography by Virginia Woolf (Harcourt, Brace, 1940)

Top A covered cup of gold, enamel and Silesian jade from Bohemia, early seventeenth century. *Above* One of Morgan's bronzes – a galloping fawn

A late eighteenth- or nineteenth-century
Venetian andiron with the figure of Venus

Two details from the Mazarin Tapestry (see pp. 78–9)

Washington. 'We had a good lunch – lots of smart women and Elihu Root. . . . Morgan, rather jovial and making jokes, which I parried, about my becoming an American. After lunch a cigar called The Regalia de Morgan.'*

Morgan, seen by Fry at close quarters, was not prepossessing. 'I don't think he wants anything but flattery', he wrote home. 'He is quite indifferent to the real value of things. All he wants experts for is to give him a sense of his own wonderful sagacity.'** 'He would make a splendid portrait like Ghirlandaio's Strozzi man in the Louvre', Fry observed, adding, 'He behaves not as a host but exactly as a crowned head and everyone else behaves accordingly.'*

Fry was one of the first to recognize the merit of the Post-Impressionists. In 1910 an exhibition of their paintings was opened at the Grafton Galleries in London. The London *Times* condemned the show and severely criticized Fry for lending his authority to the exhibition. *The Times* was supported by the great majority of critics, including Wilfrid Blunt, who wrote of the paintings, 'They are the works of idleness and of impotent stupidity, a pornographic show.'

As a result of his stand Fry, in the words of his biographer, Virginia Woolf, became 'the father of British painting and the leader of the rebels'. Besides being a distinguished critic Fry was a painter of some distinction, a lecturer and the author of many important books on art. In one of his essays he wrote:

> It is a fine point . . . whether culture is more inimical to art than barbarism, or vice versa. Culture . . . tends to keep a tradition in existence, but just when the tradition thus carefully tended through some winter of neglect begins to show signs of life by putting out new shoots and blossoms, culture must needs do its best to destroy them. As the guardian and worshipper of the dead trunk, it tries to wipe off such . . . excrescences, unable as it is to recognize in them the signs of life.

And: 'Picture galleries and museums are Temples of Culture, not of Art. . . . The devotees of culture often acquire more merit by what they know about the history of a work of art than by what they feel in front of it.'

Letters of Roger Fry, edited by Denys Sutton (Random House, 1973)

**Roger Fry: A Biography*

Two fifteenth-century maiolica plates

133

A copper gilt reliquary in the shape of the
Virgin and Child, from Spain, twelfth century

Fry, though tempted by the opportunities provided by the Metropolitan, which he believed had more money at its disposal than any museum in the world, hesitated about taking the post. He wrote of Morgan, 'The man is so swollen with pride and a sense of power that it never occurs to him that other people have any rights.' Fry decided to say no. But Morgan, showing no evidence of hyper-sensitivity or swollen pride, took no offence partly, perhaps, because first-rate experts were scarce. He made Fry the official European buying agent for the Metropolitan and gave him great freedom. Meanwhile, Fry had been offered the top post in the National Gallery of London. After an agony of indecision he finally accepted the Metropolitan offer and became the curator of paintings. He believed that art would become an American preoccupation and wrote: 'There is going to be an immense boom here in art – everything is shaping and arranging itself for it and I am regarded as the person who can give the direction to it in lots of ways.'*

His first article in the museum bulletin outlined the gaps in the picture collection. There was 'only one aspect of the art which is adequately represented', he wrote, 'and that is the sentimental and anecdotic side of nineteenth century painting – we have as yet no Byzantine paintings, no Giotto, no Giottoesque, no Mantegna, no Botticelli, no Leonardo, no Raphael, no Michelangelo. The student of the history of art must either travel in Europe or apply himself to reproductions.'

The Metropolitan trustees were primarily interested in what Fry called 'exceptional and spectacular pieces'. His inclination was to supplement such acquisitions with pictures that were good but not fashionable, a category in which he included the still highly controversial French Impressionists. In 1907 Fry persuaded Edward Robinson, the Metropolitan's assistant director, to buy a magnificent Renoir. Although it cost less than $20,000, the conservative trustees were nearly speechless with indignation. Whether Morgan agreed with this view is not known, but his vast collection contained few examples of French Impressionists.** At all events, Fry's acquisitions intensified the ill feeling between him and Morgan. This was mainly one-sided, Fry

*Letters of Roger Fry
**Perhaps Morgan was influenced by Joseph Duveen, who had decided at this time that modern pictures were cutting into his capital funds. He advised his clients not to buy any, and offered instead, at very high prices, eighteenth-century English portraits.

Adoration of the Shepherds by the Flemish painter Marcellus Coffermans,
mid-sixteenth century

136

A Flemish triptych showing the Last Supper, with Abraham receiving bread and
wine from the high priest Melchizedek, and the Fall of Manna, *c.* 1520

St Nicholas of Tolentino Reviving the Birds
by Benvenuto Tisi da Garofalo, sixteenth century

THE INCREDIBLE PIERPONT MORGAN

Warrior on Horseback (detail), from the workshop of Riccio

St John Baptizing, by Sangallo

having reached the conclusion that the chief obstacle to the museum's professional development was its president. Morgan's unilateral buying, without the knowledge of the museum's staff, threw them all into confusion; they had to scurry around to find the money to pay for the president's purchases.

Sometimes Fry accompanied Morgan on buying trips abroad; but he resented every minute and poured out his feelings in his letters. He describes Morgan as boorish and as spending money like a *nouveau riche* bourgeois. There is no evidence that Morgan was aware of Fry's seething resentment; Morgan did not write personal letters, preferring the telegraph or the telephone.

John G. Johnson, a Philadelphia collector whom Morgan had brought to the Metropolitan's board of trustees, agreed with Fry that Morgan's one-man rule had its drawbacks. 'The trouble is', he wrote Fry, 'that everyone is under the coercion of Mr Morgan's dominating will. No one does, or dares, resist it.' His will was like a force of nature, implacable and impervious to mere human disturbances.

Morgan would buy, sometimes for himself, sometimes for the museum. In London he stopped one day at Kleinburger's gallery and made an offer for a fine Fra Angelico. A few days later he received a letter from Fry, saying, 'I think I ought to tell you that I saw it [the Fra Angelico] a few days before you did, and thinking it of the utmost importance to the museum and also likely to be snapped up, I bought it.' The inference that Morgan had tried to undercut the museum was clear. 'The most remarkable letter I ever received', he observed; 'I do not propose to answer it.' Morgan never did answer it, nor did he ever mention the incident to Fry, but his displeasure was so evident that the director of the Metropolitan advised Fry to resign; the trustees then voted to terminate his appointment. Fry wrote bitterly to his father: 'Morgan would not forgive me for trying to get that picture for the museum . . . it is useless to make any fuss about it. I could get no satisfaction from these people and they have behaved vilely.'

In 1905 the distinguished art dealer, Jacques Seligmann, had his first face-to-face encounter with Morgan – at the Hotel Bristol in Paris. Not only was he kept waiting, along with a number of competitors, but the fine porcelains he had brought were rejected by Morgan. Irked, Seligmann said he would take the porcelains back provided that he was told whether Mr Morgan had simply changed his mind or whether

Meissen group: The Heart Seller, by Kändler

he challenged the authenticity of the porcelains.

At this point Morgan became irritated and red-faced; he pounded the table and roared. He told Seligmann that the reason for his refusal to accept the porcelains was none of his business. But Seligmann was a determined man unwilling to give up; he explained calmly that, if Morgan intended to buy fine objects, he would never succeed if he consulted half a dozen people about each purchase. Such a course, he said, would only result in dealers working together and arranging commissions with each other.*

This plain talk impressed Morgan but he did not change his mind. Seligmann's parting words were, 'Mr Morgan, I will see you shortly in New York and prove to you that you have been misled, but not by me.'

Realizing that his reputation might be at stake, Seligmann showed the porcelains to many specialists. He gave them to the Metropolitan Museum, where they were accepted with delight. Then he called on Morgan and won his most important American client. Seligmann became the adviser upon whom Morgan mainly relied in his later years. Morgan bought from Seligmann an unparalleled collection of Rouen faience and forty-three pieces of exquisite Byzantine enamels. In one of those charming gestures of which he was capable, he presented two of them to the Louvre.

He made another fine gesture in connection with a historic and beautiful vestment which had been presented to the cathedral at Ascoli by Pope Nicholas IV in 1288. The vestment was much admired when exhibited in London as 'the property of a great American collector', who was identified as Morgan. When asked where he had obtained this treasure, Morgan said he *thought* it might have come from Paris, but back in Ascoli some clues turned up. There the *carabinieri* revealed that the vestment had been sold by its custodians. Five priests and a photographer named Rocchiggiani were arrested. Rocchiggiani cut short his confession by hanging himself in jail.

During this turmoil it seemed all Italy was praying for the cape's return. The Italian Embassy in London took the direct approach, asking Morgan to return it, and a subscription was started in Italy to buy it back. Morgan settled the matter by returning the cape as a donation to the Italian Government.

Merchants of Art by Germain Seligman (Appleton–Century–Crofts, 1961).

Central panel of a triptych, showing the family of St Anne

Three eleventh-century Byzantine medallions from a set which was on an ikon of St Gabriel, formerly in the old church of a monastery at Jumati in Georgia. They represent Christ, St John the Baptist and St Paul.

144

A Venetian enamel glass bottle

Morgan bought lavishly from dealers, antiquaries and impoverished aristocrats. One score of bills from Paris for April and May 1906 came to $770,627. He would buy a Louis XVI gold box for $21,650 as casually as a commuter picks up a morning paper; moments later he would spend $200,000 for a Cellini cup.

An audience enhanced his pleasure. He was in too great a hurry and too imperious to bargain; he would say to a dealer, 'I've heard enough. I'll take it for what you paid, plus fifteen per cent' (not ten per cent as Fry reported). But he also refused many offers; when he paid exorbitant prices, he knew what he was doing.

Among the experts he hired was Robert Langton Douglas, an authority on Sienese paintings, from whom Morgan bought some of his best at low prices at a time when gold-background primitives were only beginning to be in vogue. But his closest adviser was Belle da Costa Greene. A charming, slim-waisted young woman with slanting, heavily lidded green eyes who looked like a Chinese firedog, she started working for Morgan in 1905 at the age of twenty-two. Sharp-tongued, quick-tempered, hot-blooded. she guarded his treasures against the wily art and book dealers and against the slurs of the malcontents. Previously under-librarian at Princeton, she came to be called 'Belle of the Books'. As Morgan's librarian she enjoyed great prestige with the book dealers and, in time, with dealers in works of art. Morgan took her opinion, even when contrary to his, like a lamb. He rarely bought anything without her approval.

Morgan used the West Room of the Library with its brocade walls bearing the coat of arms of the Chigi family of Florence. The assurance of Renaissance man faced him in a Castagno portrait and the loveliness of Renaissance woman was represented by Ghirlandaio's *Giovanna Tornabuoni*. On the walls blue-robed madonnas kept company with exquisite busts and bas-reliefs, a ruby-red K'ang Hsi vase, and pirouetting Tanagra figures. In the corner, the door opened on a hall which held the precious manuscripts and jewelled bindings.

Belle Greene, frank and often indiscreet, was the passionately loyal confidante in the West Room. She had strong prejudices. Of Bernard Berenson she wrote in a letter to Sydney Cockerell, then Director of the Fitzwilliam Museum in Cambridge, England:* '. . . like your friend, B.B.,

*The letters from Belle Greene to Sydney Cockerell were lent to the author by Mrs Sherman Haight.

Belle Greene and part of her domain
– the West Room of Morgan's
Library

Inside the Library

irritating and annoying . . . I have rarely heard him say a decent word for *anybody*, except some pretty lady. B.B.'s *pretences* are one of the things I hate most about him – someone truly said of him that he is a poisonous person.' Hard on Berenson, since he was said to have been madly in love with Belle Greene. And she with him (presumably after further acquaintance!).

148

A portrait of Giovanna Tornabuoni by Ghirlandaio

The Wool Winder by Greuze

The Temptation by Pietro Longhi

Morgan's death devastated her. In a letter with a heavy black border she poured out her grief: 'I feel as if life had stopped . . . it is all I can do to go on without him. He was much more than my "boss". He was almost a father to me. . . . So you can see I feel stranded and desolate.'

A Syrian mosque lamp, *c.* 1286

Nevertheless, she kept on working as hard and efficiently as ever. For a while she did not know whether Pierpont, Jr, would keep the library going. but he was soon infected with her buoyant enthusiasm for works of art and became her strong supporter. In a letter dated 1922 Belle writes, apparently seriously, 'J.P. Jr has been, and still is, very, very poor.'

Belle Greene ruled the library, Morgan's favourite and most apposite environment. She was, according to one of the library's catalogues, 'no conventional librarian of fiction, gliding rubber heeled with finger to lips . . . [her] work was carried on heartily, noisily, in a whirl of books and papers disturbing to one who could not perceive the cosmic order-liness of purpose which underlay the surface confusion.' In fact she was an extraordinary woman; glamorous and heavily perfumed, and dressed in Renaissance gowns adorned with matching jewels. She was imperious in manner: she once remarked, 'If a person is a worm, you step on him.' On trips abroad, made on Mr Morgan's behalf, she would take along her thoroughbred horse which she rode in Hyde Park. Jacques Seligmann said of her, 'She was young and slender, quick in her movement, and already well established in the reputation for "le mot juste" which has made her something of a legend in the world of art.'

The many letters from Belle Greene to Cockerell reveal her warmth and humour; they are mainly concerned with rare manuscripts but contain much shrewd observation. Very well expressed, they are full of underlinings – like Queen Victoria's – and it is curious how Belle's handwriting changes. She had two entirely different scripts.

She and Cockerell evidently became intimate friends; occasionally she ends a letter with 'yours eternally'. She twits him now and then: 'Are you nice and chubby, or are you just dull?' And there are surprises, as when she refers to Fry as 'that nice man'; for it was Fry who hated Morgan and treated him so shabbily. She calls Seymour de Ricci (a widely known French bibliophile) 'that dreadful Dr Ricci'. Concerning a stay in Florence she writes: 'I spent three days with the Berensons at Settignano. They had a highly intellectual house party which rather got on my nerves with its "precious" atmosphere.'

One of her most delightful letters to Cockerell relates an anecdote about a man she encountered:

> I had a most screamingly funny proposal of 'honest marriage' the other day – [from] a Western lumberman who is conceded to be one of the richest men in the country. He . . . put himself and his checkbook in my hands – so we did luncheons, dinners, theaters, joy rides, all the museums, not to mention dealers – for I made him buy a Reynolds, a Raeburn and a Gainsborough . . . and (don't laugh) a private railroad car! Then, after he had been back about a fortnight, along comes a telegram – 'When will you marry me? . . . Reply pd. . . .' I sent word that all such proposals would be considered alphabetically after my 50th birthday.

Belle Greene was described as 'flamboyant only in trivial things', such as insisting on having the best seat in the theatre, ordering a particular dish in a restaurant and getting rid of a bore. But her talents were formally recognized. Twice in one year she turned down honorary degrees; one from the University of California. In 1921, at a time when women were not prominent, she was awarded the French Government's 'Palme d'Officier de l'Instruction Publique'; she also received honours from other foreign governments.

The Ventriloquist, made of French porcelain

A Ch'ing dynasty vase

Morgan was so formidable that few dealers dared to cheat him; there were, however, attempts at fraud. Berenson told with malicious delight the story of a painting at a London dealer's which had been 'faked up' from a Ghirlandaio to a Raphael. According to Berenson the dealer said, 'Mr Morgan, all the critics say this is not a Raphael, but you know it is.' Morgan replied, 'Wrap it up.' He often went shopping without an adviser and made impetuous purchases; but his percentage of mistakes was very small. Experience was a good teacher.

Morgan was not the megalomaniacal, Hearstian type of collector; he was, rather, the true patrician, to the art-manner born. As Frederick Lewis Allen observed, it was his nature to pursue 'the life of an un-ostentatious man on a majestic scale.' He collected because he enjoyed shopping; his sensitivity to beauty was inborn. His taste was catholic, but although he cherished Oriental porcelains, he vetoed other art from the Orient.

When the Metropolitan Museum sent a group of archaeologists to Egypt, Morgan decided that they should have something better than a tent to live in. Accordingly, he had built a large, comfortable base headquarters. The diggings, south of Cairo, were under the supervision of Albert Lythgoe, who got on famously with Morgan. A vast amount of material was excavated and the Metropolitan's Egyptian collection became outstanding.

The museum also acquired some fine armour. One of the trustees, Rutherford Stuyvesant, when in Paris, snared the collection of the Duc de Dino. Morgan had learned that the duke, being short of cash, in-tended to sell his collection of armour at auction. Dino told Stuyvesant that he would take $240,000 for his armour; Stuyvesant then wrote a cheque for this amount without mentioning that there were not suffi-cient funds in his account at the Crédit Lyonnais. Fearing that any delay might cause the duke to change his mind, Stuyvesant cabled Morgan in New York. The message arrived at 3 A.M. and Morgan immediately called a meeting of the museum's trustees in his Library. The inevitable shakedown ensued, with Morgan telling each man how much he should contribute (they were later reimbursed by the Rogers Fund). The entire collection of the Duc de Dino arrived at the Metro-politan in 1904.

After Morgan's semi-retirement in 1907 it was more or less assumed that his entire collection, enormously larger than Altman's, would be

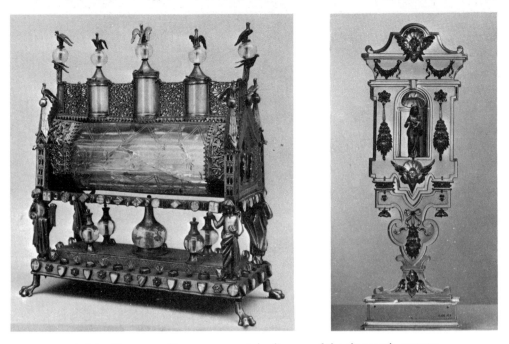

Left La Chasse aux Oiseaux – a crystal reliquary of the thirteenth century
Right An early seventeenth-century crystal shrine

left to the Metropolitan, but no one had dared put the matter to him directly. He clearly relished being president and was a considerate one in many ways. For example, at one of the formal receptions for members, he and the other trustees were surprised to see a young woman who was carrying a baby. She was the wife of a museum attendant 'who knew no better'. 'Morgan shook hands with her as graciously as he did with a lady in full evening dress', Robert De Forest, a trustee, reported admiringly; 'and, as she passed by, he said to me, "Quick, get that baby's name so that I can make him a life member of the museum."' Morgan not only put up $1000 to make the infant (it happened to be a girl) a life member, but also set aside $500 more so that she could study art in Europe when she grew up.

In later life Morgan would spend half the year abroad, accompanied by a retinue of servants, art experts, relatives and usually a charming female companion. These people helped to insulate him from the army of dealers, impoverished aristocrats and confidence men who laid siege to his hotel as he travelled grandly from London to Paris, to Aix-les-Bains, Monte Carlo, Rome and Venice. Each one had something for his eyes alone and Morgan would exclaim that the most expensive words in any language were *unique au monde*.

157

VIII

MORGAN THE COLLECTOR – POST-PRINCES GATE

MORGAN KEPT the bulk of his purchases at his house in London, at Princes Gate. Some European countries made it difficult to export works of art, and the United States, by imposing duty of twenty per cent,* made it more difficult to bring them in. Even for Morgan, whose collections immediately after his death were valued by *The Times* of London at $60 million, the duty would have been prohibitive. Morgan was, of course, too honourable to consider any kind of tax evasion, but some other collectors were less scrupulous. Joseph Widener, for instance, bought some magnificent Van Dyck portraits abroad, and allowed them to be rolled up and stuffed into false automobile exhaust pipes to get them through the Italian customs.

Morgan placed a number of his finest treasures at the Victoria and Albert and other London museums. In 1909, however, the United States abolished the import duty on works of art more than one hundred years old and heavy death duties were imposed in England; these actions changed the situation. Accordingly, Morgan set in motion the vast process of packing and shipping his collections to America; as the cases arrived they were taken to the Metropolitan and stored there. The general assumption that they would stay put was soon rudely shattered.

The Morgan treasures left England in 1912. Among them were fourteen Fragonard paintings, which had been commissioned by the Comtesse Du Barry. According to S. N. Behrman the lady had refused them because of her objection to one called *Storming the Citadel* as being too forthright a comment on her relations with the king. 'She didn't mind being a citadel,' he says, 'and she didn't even mind being stormed but she didn't want it suggested to posterity that the citadel had fallen.'

Robert De Forest, by now vice president of the Metropolitan, placed a note of clarification in the museum bulletin about the disposal of the

---

*In *Secrets of an Art Dealer* (E. P. Dutton & Co., 1938) James Henry Duveen puts the duty at sixty per cent.

158

A leaf of a medieval ivory diptych

DNS LOQVITVR MARIE

Morgan Collection. It was true, he wrote, that it was being transferred to New York, but 'of Mr Morgan's further intentions we have no knowledge'. It would be a 'pleasant dream' if he decided to place it permanently with the Metropolitan – 'nor would it be out of line with Mr Morgan's never-failing public spirit if this dream should come true.' But this could happen only if the museum had space to show the collection, and, as De Forest noted, 'it has no such space now.'

De Forest was touching on a tricky situation. Under the Metropolitan's charter all construction funds came from the city, which so far had failed to appropriate the money needed for more gallery space. The city authorities felt that if Morgan wished to immortalize himself by leaving his collections to New York, he could well afford to pay for their accommodation. Morgan was amazed and summoned Edward Robinson, the director, to his house. Robinson's memorandum of the meeting, dated 29 November 1912, pictures it as an unhappy occasion; Morgan said that he had no intention of giving or bequeathing his collections to the Metropolitan. He added that, as he estimated their value at $50 million (this sum must be multiplied many times to take into account today's art prices and the current value of the dollar), he regarded this asset as much too large to take out of his estate, in case it should ever be needed.

Morgan left his art collections to his son, J. Pierpont Morgan, Jr, stating in his will his 'desire and intention to make some suitable disposition of them or of such portions of them – which would render them permanently available for the instruction and pleasure of the American people.'

He had been too proud to buy himself space in the Metropolitan when the city refused to put up the money for a new wing. But, ironically, when the Board of Estimate finally relented, the need of the Morgan estate for cash intervened. In this connection, John D. Rockefeller, Sr, recalling that it was Morgan who successfully ended the Panic of 1907, remarked: 'And to think that he wasn't even a rich man.'

In 1914 Morgan's son authorized the trustees of the Metropolitan to exhibit his father's collection in its entirety; it filled the second floor of the newly opened northernmost Fifth Avenue wing. This was the only time that the Morgan Collection has ever been seen as a whole; many of the finest works of art had to be sold thereafter to meet demands on the estate. Henry Clay Frick paid $1,200,000 for five of the Fragonard

A Lady Writing by Vermeer

Gallery Sixteen of the Metropolitan's exhibition of the Morgan Collection in 1914.
The tapestries are Flemish (made after 1520) and show the story of Noah.

panels; they had cost Morgan $310,000 in 1899. The designation, 'ex-Morgan pieces', became a seal of quality and desirability so that collectors would buy them as they would 'Medici' paintings. It was Belle Greene who saw to it that Morgan items, sold after his death, fetched good prices, and it was she who built up his son's interest in the library.

Although the Morgan collection – the greatest in modern times – was widely dispersed, about forty per cent of it came to rest in the Metropolitan. J. P. Morgan, Jr, presented the museum with his father's treasures in successive years, and the 1917 gift alone comprised six to eight thousand objects, ranging from Raphael's Colonna Altarpiece, which cost Morgan $484,000, to gold, diamond and enamel eighteenth-century boxes by the dozen, paintings, sculpture, Egyptian and Assyrian material, Byzantine ivories and Gothic woodcarvings. All this was exhibited in the Decorative Arts Wing, where it was supposed to be kept together as a unit for the next half-century; but some years later Morgan, Jr, consented to the distribution of objects throughout the museum. Other segments of the collection are in the Wadsworth Atheneum in Hartford and scattered in other museums.

Headed for the horror of World War I, the world that Pierpont Morgan knew did not long survive his death. It was the artists, as usual,

162

Above Gallery Eighteen. The tapestry on the left was woven in the Beauvais Manufactory in 1733. The other three are part of a set of five Gobelin tapestries illustrating the story of Don Quixote.
Below Gallery Fifteen. From the left, the paintings are by Rembrandt (see p. 121), Rubens (*The Archduke Ferdinand*) and Van Dyck (*The Earl of Warwick*).

who were the first to sense the violence to come – men like Marcel Duchamp, Picasso and Kandinsky were creating a different kind of art. Years passed before this new painting could be seen at the Metropolitan; Morgan's influence continued for a long time during which the museum considered itself a bulwark against the 'curse' of modernism. Yet it was Morgan who helped to bring on the popular success of art in our time.

Francis Henry Taylor compares Morgan as a collector with Lorenzo de' Medici, although Morgan did not approach Lorenzo in the support of contemporary talent. Taylor wrote: 'Both men looked upon money as a source of maximum power and infallibility – never as an end in itself. And both induced in their contemporaries a new attitude toward the significance of works of art.' Morgan was by no means the first prominent American to collect art, but no one else made collecting so exciting an occupation.

Francis Leland, a large donor to the Metropolitan, told Edward Robinson that he thought 'the bringing of the Morgan collections to America the greatest event that had ever happened to any country.' The Morgan Collection represents the grandest gesture of *noblesse oblige* the world has known. In the words of Francis Henry Taylor: 'Pierpont Morgan was the greatest figure in the art world that America has yet produced, a visionary and a patron such as we never knew before, nor ever shall again.'

In early 1913 Morgan, accompanied by his daughter Louisa and her husband, Herbert Satterlee – Mrs Morgan remained at home – went to Egypt. On their way back to New York, the party got only as far as Rome, for Morgan's health was failing. In Rome he summoned enough strength to attend an Easter service; thereafter he lost ground fast. His mind went back to Hartford and school in Switzerland. The last words his son-in-law heard him say were, 'I've got to go up the hill.' Later that day, 31 March 1913, aged not quite seventy-six years, Morgan died. His body was taken back to New York, where a great funeral was held at St George's. He was buried in Hartford with his father and mother.

What was the legacy of Pierpont Morgan, beyond his art collection, his fortune and the great enterprises he established? What he essentially left for American posterity was a tradition of uncompromising honesty. The last towering individual in American business, he was the last of the financial Titans – a man who knew what he wanted and got it.

Morgan lives on as a gigantic figure of his time.

A NOTE ON MORGAN'S CHILDREN

ORGAN'S SON, J. Pierpont, Jr, looked like his father but although his career as a banker was outstanding his business methods were quite different. He was a quiet, able person who gave the impression of being an Englishman. Under his guidance J. P. Morgan & Company carried on successfully, and he and his brilliant partners – Henry P. Davison, Thomas W. Lamont, Dwight Morrow, Russell Leffingwell and George Whitney – maintained the Morgan tradition of fair dealing. J. P. Morgan & Company continued to take risks. In 1914 the firm gambled on the Allies winning the war, just as Junius Morgan, J. Pierpont Jr's grandfather, had done in the Franco-Prussian War of 1870. It was the Morgan group that financed the vast shipment of arms to France and England.

Anne Morgan resembled her father in character and personality more than any of his other children. A woman of unusual force, she achieved fame for organizing French relief during World War I, and after the war continued to help France through rehabilitation of the wounded. Back in New York, Anne Morgan, who never married, developed a slum area into Sutton Place and so started the beautification of the East River front. She was an extraordinarily generous person, always ready to help friends in need; she bought paintings she did not really want because she felt the artists deserved support. Her expenditures were so great that she finally had to sell her fine house on Sutton Place.

Morgan's daughter Louisa, Mrs Herbert Satterlee, in contrast to Anne, was self-effacing like her mother, who quietly ran the various Morgan establishments and provided a perfect partner for her dominating husband. Her sister Juliet, who married William Pierson Hamilton, was a positive person. Even at the age of six she attracted attention – as when, from a window of a steamer her father had chartered for a trip up the Nile, she waved to a crowd of Arab natives, kissing her hands and laughing. She was very pretty as well as vivacious.

165

Morgan loved children, particularly his granddaughter Mabel Satterlee, and the Morgan family life was pleasantly harmonious. In quiet surroundings – Cragston, like the other Morgan establishments, had an easy informality – the pace was slow, unlike that of the master of the house as he avidly pursued his meteoric Wall Street career.

Morgan with two of his grown children, Louisa and Jack

166

APPENDIX:
A NOTE ON THE MORGAN COLLECTION*

THE RANGE and catholicity of these assemblages from all periods and civilizations are staggering to the imagination. Ancient art in its most disparate styles and techniques from 3000 B.C. to the fifth century A.D., including six large alabaster Assyrian reliefs from the palace of Ashur-nasir-pal at Nimrod; an assortment running into the hundreds of minor antiquities, seals and jewels from Egypt, Greece and the Aegean lands; sculpture of the Eighteenth Dynasty, and the Gréau Collection of ancient glass numbering over eight hundred items; silver dishes from Cyprus and the golden bowls of the Alban treasure; two collections of Gallo-Roman, Germanic, and Merovingian art consisting of personal ornaments of the barbaric tribes from the fall of the Roman Empire to the time of Charlemagne – the one gathered throughout France by Stanislas Baron, and the other assembled from excavations made by the German antiquary Queckenberg at Niederbreisig between Coblenz and Bonn.

These artifacts alone would bring any museum to the front rank but, taken in conjunction with the incredible sequences of hundreds of Byzantine and Romanesque objects for devotional use and domestic ornament, they suddenly placed the Metropolitan, when they were ultimately received there, on a footing with the Cluny and the Victoria and Albert museums. To these were added specialized groups of comparable importance: Renaissance jewels and ornaments from every country; the Le Breton Collection of faience from Rouen, Moustiers, Marseilles, and other French centers; the Marfels Collection of watches; and the Gutmann Collection of antique plate and bronzes of German Renaissance and Baroque workmanship. These are but a few of the various lots which were swept into the tidal wave of Morgan's enthusiasm.

*From *Pierpont Morgan As Collector and Patron* by Francis Henry Taylor (The Pierpont Morgan Library, 1970)

NOTES ON THE COLOR PLATES

33   Detail showing the upper half of a plaque from an altar frontal. Champlevé enamel with applied figure (St James). French (Limoges), second half of thirteenth century. *The Metropolitan Museum of Art; Gift of J. Pierpont Morgan, 1917*

34   Dutch painting, *A Visit to the Nursery*, by Gabriel Metsu (1629–67). Oil on canvas, 30½ in. × 32 in. Signed and dated (over door, left): G. Metsu 1661. *The Metropolitan Museum of Art; Gift of J. Pierpont Morgan, 1917*

51   Folio 11 of *Manafi al-Hayawan* ('Advantages Derived from Animals'), a manuscript written and illuminated in Persian. Illustration of lion and lioness (note birds). The original Arabic text was translated into Persian by Abd al-Hadi bin Muhammad bin Mahmud bin Ibrahim at the order of the Mongol ruler of Persia, Ghazan Khan, (1294–1305). The present MS. was written *c.* 1295 at Maragha near Tabris, Persia, (an important cultural centre in the thirteenth century) for Shams ad-Din ibn Juja ad-Din al-Zushaki, of whom nothing is known. Purchased in 1912 from P. M. Turner. *The Pierpont Morgan Library*

52   The Duff-Ogilvie portrait of Mary, Queen of Scots (1542–87), with her son, James VI (1566–1625), afterwards James I of England. Artist unknown, sixteenth century, oil on stone, 8⅞ in. × 7¾ in. *The Metropolitan Museum of Art; Gift of J. Pierpont Morgan, 1917*

77 top   Pendant jewel, with a *commesso* showing Prudence with a mirror and serpent, of carved white chalcedony, tooled and enamelled gold, with diamonds and ruby. The reverse shows Diana of the Hunt and hounds, in translucent coloured enamel. Openwork frame, enamelled and set with rubies and emeralds and hung with a pendant pearl. Design after Charles Etienne Delaune (1518/19 – prob. 1583), court artist to Henry II of France. French (Fontaineblue), 1550–5. Height: 3½ in. *The Metropolitan Museum of Art; Gift of J. Pierpont Morgan, 1917*

77 bottom   Chasse or reliquary of champlevé enamel on copper. French (Limoges), end twelfth

or beginning thirteenth century. *The Metropolitan Museum of Art; Gift of J. Pierpont Morgan, 1917*

78–9   The Mazarin Tapestry, named after Cardinal Mazarin, is believed to be the product of Flemish artisans working in Brussels between 1495 and 1500, probably in the studio of Jan van Roome. It represents the Triumph of Christ, a theme based on the last book of the New Testament, *The Revelation of Saint John the Divine*. Although it is not known who commissioned the tapestry, it may celebrate a historic marriage (between Anne of Brittany and Charles VIII of France in 1491 or, more likely, Joanna the Mad of Spain and Philip the Handsome of Burgundy in 1496). Wool and silk with gold and silver threads. Height: 134 in.; width: 158 in. *Widener Collection* (ex-collection J. P. Morgan) *National Gallery of Art, Washington, D.C.*

80   Folio 6v from a Book of Hours. Illustration for the month of May: boating party (note the wine cooler trailing in the water). Early sixteenth century, Belgian. *The Pierpont Morgan Library*

105   Folio 2 of *De Spiritu Sancto* by Didymus Alexandrinus, translated by St Jerome. Florence, 1488. Incipit page showing St Jerome with the city of Florence in the background; *left* (in red, kneeling) King Corvinus facing Beatrice of Aragon (kneeling) *right*. King Corvinus of Hungary was the patron for whom the book was made. Following his death, Beatrice of Aragon returned to Italy, taking some of their library, including *De Spiritu Sancto* with her. This book was later acquired by Louise Charlotte de Bourbon, daughter of Lodovico, Duke of Parma, and bequeathed by her in 1855 to the Jesuit College at Wien-Lainz. In 1912 it was purchased by Morgan from Alexander Imbert. *The Pierpont Morgan Library*

106   Ship with silver-gilt hull and oval base embossed with waves and dolphins; foliated stem with scrolls; silver sails, crow's nest, pennant and rigging; six figures and two cannon on deck; two figures climbing rigging. German (Nuremberg), early seventeenth century, made by Esaias zur Linden (master 1609, died 1632). Height: 19⅝ in.;

length: $8\frac{1}{2}$ in. Ex-coll. J. and C. Jeidels, Frankfurt am Main; Gutmann, Berlin. *The Metropolitan Museum of Art; Gift of J. Pierpont Morgan, 1917*

123   French painting, *The Swing*, by Hubert Robert (1733–1808). One of six paintings that were decorations for a boudoir in the Château de Bagatelle, near Paris. Oil on canvas, $68\frac{1}{4}$ in. × $34\frac{5}{8}$ in. Signed (on base of statue): H. Robert. *The Metropolitan Museum of Art; Gift of J. Pierpont Morgan. 1917*

124   Statuette of the Visitation, polychromed wood and gilt, set with cabochons. Height: $23\frac{1}{4}$ in.; width: 12 in. Attributed to Master Heinrich of Constance. German, early fourteenth century (c. 1310). *The Metropolitan Museum of Art; Gift of J. Pierpont Morgan, 1917*

141   The Heart Seller by Johann Joachim Kändler (1706–75). Meissen, porcelain. *Wadsworth Atheneum, Hartford, Connecticut; Gift of J. Pierpont Morgan*

142   Triptych (detail, centre panel): Family of St Anne. From the atelier of Jean Pénicaud II. Sold by Charles Stein of Paris to J. Pierpont Morgan at his sale at Galerie Georges Petit, June 1899. Acquired by the Frick in 1916. *Copyright The Frick Collection, New York*

159   Leaf of a diptych. Upper register: The Journey to Emmaus; one disciple carries a mantle and water bottle on a staff over his shoulder; the other rests on his staff and raises his hand in amazement. Lower register: the 'Noli me tangere'; legend above figures (the Lord talks to Mary). Spanish, mid-twelfth century. Ivory. Height: $10\frac{5}{8}$ in.; width: $5\frac{5}{16}$ in. *The Metropolitan Museum of Art, Gift of J. Pierpont Morgan, 1917*

160   Dutch painting, *A Lady Writing*, by Jan Vermeer (1632–75). Oil on canvas, $17\frac{3}{4}$ in. × $15\frac{3}{4}$ in., c. 1665. Acquired by Morgan in Paris in 1907. *Gift of Harry Waldron Havemeyer and Horace Havemeyer, Jr, in memory of their father Horace Havemeyer, to the National Gallery of Art, Washington, D.C.*

LIST AND SOURCES OF MONOCHROME ILLUSTRATIONS

The following abbreviations are used in the list:
Satterlee – pictures taken from *The Life of J. Pierpont Morgan* (privately printed, 1937) and *J. Pierpont Morgan: An Intimate Portrait* (Macmillan, 1939), both by Herbert L. Satterlee, by kind permission of Mrs Mabel S. Ingalls and Mr Henry S. Morgan
Frick – The Frick Collection, New York
LC – Library of Congress, Washington, D.C.
Mansell – The Mansell Collection, London
Metropolitan – The Metropolitan Museum of Art, New York; Gift of J. Pierpont Morgan, 1917
RTHPL – The Radio Times Hulton Picture Library, London
WA – Western Americana Picture Library, Brentwood, Essex

The illustrations are listed from top to bottom and left to right.

BIBLIOGRAPHY

ALLEN, Frederick Lewis, *The Great Pierpont Morgan*, N.Y., Harper & Brothers, 1949

--- *The Lords of Creation*, N.Y., Harper & Brothers, 1935

AMORY, Cleveland, *Who Killed Society?*, N.Y., Harper & Brothers, 1960

ANDREWS, Wayne, *Mr Morgan and His Architect*, N.Y., The Pierpont Morgan Library, 1957

BEARD, Charles A. and Mary, *The Rise of American Civilization*, Vol. II, N.Y., Macmillan Co., 1933

BEER, Thomas, *The Mauve Decade*, N.Y., Alfred A. Knopf, 1924

BEHRMAN, S. N., *Duveen*, N.Y., Random House, 1952

--- *People in a Diary: A Memoir*, Boston, Little, Brown & Co., 1972

COREY, Lewis, *House of Morgan*, G. Howard Watt, 1930

DUVEEN, James Henry, *Secrets of an Art Dealer*, N.Y., E. P. Dutton & Co., 1938

HEVEY, Carl, *The Life Story of J. Pierpont Morgan*, Sturgis & Walton, 1911

HOLBROOK, Stewart H, *Age of the Moguls*, N.Y., Doubleday & Co., 1953

HOYT, Edwin, *The House of Morgan*, N.Y., Dodd, Mead & Co., 1967

LINDBERGH, Anne Morrow, *Bring Me a Unicorn*, N.Y., Harcourt Brace Jovanovich, 1972, and London, Chatto and Windus, 1973

MINER, Dorothy, (editor) *Studies in Art and Literature for Belle da Costa Greene*, Princeton University Press, 1954

MORRIS, Richard B., (editor) *Encyclopedia of American History*, revised edition, N.Y., Harper & Row, 1970

MOULTON, Elizabeth, *St George's Church*, privately printed, 1964

PECORA, Ferdinand, *Wall Street Under Oath*, N.Y., Simon & Schuster, 1939

RAINSFORD, W. S., *Story of a Varied Life*, N.Y., Doubleday, Page & Co., 1922

SAARINEN, Aline, *The Proud Possessors*, N.Y., Random House, 1958

SATTERLEE, Herbert L., *The Life of J. Pierpont Morgan*, privately printed, 1937

--- *J. Pierpont Morgan: An Intimate Portrait*, N.Y., Macmillan Co., 1939

SELIGMAN, Germain, *Merchants of Art*, N.Y., Appleton-Century-Crofts, 1961

STEFFENS, Lincoln, *The Autobiography of Lincoln Steffens*, N.Y., Harcourt, Brace & Co., 1931

SULLIVAN, Mark, *Our Times*, Vol. II, N.Y., Charles Scribner's Sons, 1929

SUTTON, Denys, (editor) *Letters of Roger Fry*, 2 vols, Random House, N.Y., 1973

TAYLOR, Francis Henry, *Pierpont Morgan As Collector and Patron, 1837–1913*, revised edition, N.Y., The Pierpont Morgan Library, 1970

TOMKINS, Calvin, *Merchants and Masterpieces: The Story of the Metropolitan*, N.Y., E. P. Dutton & Co., 1970

TOWNER, Wesley, *The Elegant Auctioneers*, N.Y., Hill & Wang, 1970

WASSON, Gordon, *The Hall Carbine Affair*, privately printed, 1971

WINKLER, John K., *Morgan the Magnificent*, Garden City Publishing Co., 1930

WOOLF, Virginia, *Roger Fry: A Biography*, N.Y., Harcourt, Brace & Co., 1940

Agnew's – 1817–1967, privately printed, 1967

Letters of Belle Greene to Sydney Cockerell

The files of the *New York Times*

INDEX

Page numbers in *italic* refer to illustrations
The relationships of certain people to John Pierpont Morgan, Sr,
are shown in brackets after their names

173